BEACH MONEY™

Network marketing is the distribution of products and services through a network of independent representatives. Each representative is responsible to consume and sell a small amount of product and then recruit others to do the same. Sales volume is generated through a lot of people each buying and selling a small amount of product. Commissions are paid based on training new distributors and the consumption of products and services in the network. A company offering a product or service can eliminate the need for expensive advertising campaigns by deploying a network of individuals who get paid for sharing products and services they love with others through word of mouth. An individual seeking an income opportunity can generate an unlimited stream of commissions through repeat business and sales within his or her growing organization.

BEACH MONEY™

Creating Your Dream Life Through Network Marketing

JORDAN ADLER

New and Revised Edition including Four Additional Chapters.

MOtivational PRESS®
LEADERS IN GLOBAL PUBLISHING

Published by Motivational Press, Inc.
1777 Aurora Road
Melbourne, Florida, 32935
www.MotivationalPress.com

Manufactured in the United States of America.

ISBN: 978-1-62865-449-3

*In memory of
my friend and mentor Jay Smith*

The Beach Money Legacy

Beach Money serves as a roadmap to creating long-term success in network marketing — to create professional freedom, residual income, and work that is fulfilling, while adding value to the lives of many others. Long before the book was published, Jordan decided that its purpose was to be two-fold:

• To be a call to action to the people who read it, igniting inspiration and offering guidance.

• To touch the lives of even more people, by directing the book sale profits to an exceptional cause.

KIVA is a nonprofit organization that helps individuals lend money to the working poor. Its mission is to connect people through lending for the sake of alleviating poverty. This is done by micro-

financing (giving small loans to) outstanding entrepreneurs from impoverished communities worldwide. *The Beach Money* book sale profits go to a revolving loan fund to continuously empower entrepreneurs, who may not have the economic infrastructure or freedom to enjoy network marketing, but have the passion and spirit to be in business, support their families and lift their communities from poverty. And as they pay back their loans, the money is immediately lent to the next entrepreneur.

So far, over $300,000 has been loaned through the efforts of this giving project. You are helping us reach our goal of "1 million copies sold," and in turn funding thousands of people every month, forever. Thank you for contributing to this world-changing legacy!

http://www.kiva.org/lender/beachmoney

Beach Money Update

Since Beach Money was published in 2008, it has sold over 500,000 copies and continues to sell 3,000 to 8,000 copies a month. Beach Money has taken on a life of its own all thanks to you. I was recently in Cancun, Mexico and on my second night, a young couple in their twenties came over to me and, in broken English said, "Are you Jordan Adler?" They were from Columbia and had purchased and read Beach Money. They were on a leadership retreat with 600 others from all over Latin America and most of them had read my book. Over the next 4 days I had kids from Honduras, Mexico, Columbia and Nicaragua come over to introduce themselves and take photos.

Nathan Goldberg is a friend of mine from Canada and has been rising in the ranks of his company for a number of years. He has purchased over 6000 copies of Beach Money for his team. He has one of the fastest growing teams worldwide.

In 2009, Zsuzsanna Bak went on a networking cruise and heard me speak about Beach Money. She purchased the book, read it and decided she needed to live on the beach. So two years later she moved from Europe to the Caribbean where she lives today building her network marketing business.

On Instagram there are pictures of thousands of network marketers on the beach reading Beach Money. I'm very proud of this. It makes me feel great to know that this book has touched so many lives.

Beach Money was such a hit, that I decided to publish another book with more stories and a little different perspective. After many months of deliberating over the name for a second book, I was sitting around a fire with some good friends and one of them asked me what my second book was about. I had gone through about 40 titles and some of them were good, but none of them were exactly right. I answered my friend by saying, "The only thing I can tell you is that it is better than *Beach Money*." He said, "Better than *Beach Money*?" And I said, "Yes!" Well that's where my new book got its name. It's "Better Than Beach Money." You can learn more about my new book at www.beachmoney.com.

A Short Note From the Author

This book was written for you. I purposely have not had it professionally edited because I wanted it to "read" as if I were having a personal conversation with you. If you are an educated person, that's great, but you don't need to feel you are book smart to create a large passive residual income in network marketing. I have read many books over the years that were hard to read because the authors had great writers who made them look extremely intelligent.

I would rather have you get a lot out of this book than to have you set it down and say, "That Jordan guy is really intelligent." My hopes are that you feel inspired and encouraged by the words on these pages.

All of the stories you are about to read are true. The names have not been changed. I love all the people that I have written about in this book because I have learned and continue to learn many lessons from them. They are the reason for my success and the reason this book has been written.

There is no need to take notes or try to absorb the contents of this book. You can just sit back and enjoy it. You will get exactly what you need to get from it as you read. See you on the beach!

Acknowledgments

I WANT TO THANK YOU…

You are my friends, my never-ending inspiration and my reason for writing this book. I consider each of you a major contributor. Thank you for your advice, your encouragement, your leadership, and your love. Without you, this book would not have been written.

To my mother and my father for loving me even when I didn't listen and for being my best example of stability.

To my sisters Audrey and Donna for being my best friends growing up.

To Jackie Ulmer and Judy Dubiel for helping me see in the real world what was truly possible for me through network marketing.

To Kenny and Lisa Troutt, Kody and Jodi Bateman, and BK Boreyko, for having the courage to see the job through and offering me a foundation of leadership.

To Gemma Farrell for coaching me through the process of writing this book and helping to make a lifelong dream come true.

To Megan Drescher for running my life while I'm running my businesses.

To Ivan Misner and Norm Dominguez for teaching me true networking through the examples and training set forth in their organization, Business Networking International (BNI).

To Steve Smith for showing me what it means to dream big and to keep it simple.

To Pat Hintze and Steve Schulz for helping me see that real people can make it big in network marketing.

To Russ and Ulli Johnson for a lifetime of fun in a few short years.

To Jay and Meg Smith for believing in me and being the greatest examples of integrity that I know.

To DeMarr Zimmerman for sharing with me one of the greatest opportunities of my lifetime.

To Bob and Betty Ann Golden for opening their home to me and being my perfect friends.

To Scott and Kristi Mercker for their caring thoughts.

To Chuck Brewer for being my first example of entrepreneurism.

To Jimmy Dick for encouraging me to stretch beyond my self-imposed limitations.

To Tom "Big Al" Schreiter for teaching my teams through his comical stories.

To Huel Cox for inspiring me to step into leadership.

To Jana Rengifo for being my best friend in life and an ongoing source of inspiration and love.

To the Packard family, Jim, Sherry, Jeff and Adam, for continuing to raise the bar.

To Tom Hopkins for helping me see what it means to be a professional salesperson.

To David Frey for showing me that there is more than one way to build a successful network.

To Paul Orbeson for proving that it's possible to earn one million dollars per month in network marketing.

To Al Thomas for being one of the most influential figures in my life and for teaching me the ropes about business over an occasional cigar.

To Nate and Kelley Dominguez for helping to keep my life light and fun.

To Judy O'Higgins and her entire team for demonstrating what can happen when a group of people chooses to step into greatness.

To Jerry Knight for being one of my best friends and for helping unbury me when I was up to my ears in work.

To Carrie Putman and her ladies from Bookkeeping Helpers for loving to do what I don't love to do.

To Don Mastrangelo, my co-host and mentor, for encouraging me to finally write this book.

To Chuck and Nicki Pousson for being great leaders and introducing me to many other great leaders.

To Loral Langemeier for teaching me business strategies and introducing me to some of the most amazing people I will ever meet.

To Jack Birnbaum for suggesting that I will become a better leader by replacing myself.

To Erik Laver for encouraging me to rise up to my true potential.

To Todd Falcone for calling me back!

To Chris and Josephine Gross for promoting me.

To Anissa Blanchard for propping me up when I needed it most.

To Mark Herdering for never giving up on himself!

To Russ and Mary Nolan for challenging me to get up in front of a group and share my story.

To Jerry Haines for introducing me to Jim Packard.

To John and Patrice Jones for demonstrating the power of faith.

To Don from University and Hardy for opening my eyes.

To Kim Butler for preparing me for my success.

To Scott Pospichal for creating some of the best memories of my life.

To Ines Kinchen for being my cheerleader and my loving book advisor.

To my cousin Eddie for being the brother I never had.

To Bill Lyons for teaching me to passionately pursue my

dreams.

To Daniel and Bhavna Dreher for showing me the Law of Attraction in action.

To Warren Taryle for his creative genius and for showing me how really interesting accounting and taxes can be.

To Chuck and Sandra Hoover for paving the way and keeping it fun.

To Chuck Brewer for being my first real exposure to entrepreneurship and his wife Lori for leading me back to Chuck.

To Coach Mellema for inspiring me to push beyond my self-imposed limitations.

To David Rita for co-signing on my first loan and giving me a floor to sleep on!

To Tommy Wyatt and Curtis Lewsey for bringing true network marketing back to the team.

To Melody Marler Forshee for helping to take Beach Money to new heights.

I would also like to thank Sprock, Jishelle, Dan and Jenny, Randy, Shay, Dianna, Art and Ann, Chip, Tom, Laura, Larry, Chad, Phil and Sheila, D'vorah, Kathy, Bobby and Sara, Michael, the Mims, Dale, Chrissy, Nancy, Eric and Barb, Heather and Mike, Shawn, Adrian and Lyndi, Jeremy and Adrian, Lizzy, Mark and Karen, Roger, Pat and Tracy, Han, Mike and Donna, Dale, Steve, Jody, the Cross family, Robert, Noel and Anna, Senator Mike and Vivian, Dan and Judy, Chris and Lynnette, Darry, Neil, Patty and Kevin, Stan and Shirley, Chris and Dena, Gary and Sally, Martha, Eric and Maria, Lee and Rhonda, Carla, Tim, Mike and Jan, Frank and Starla, The Fonz and Penny, Jordan, Casey, Elliot, Jeffery and Erica, Arlene, Bobby, Kristi and Scott.

I honor you and thank you for helping me create the life of my dreams. Please know that I am forever grateful to you and to the people in your lives that brought you to me.

Contents

CHAPTER 1

Beach Money

When I was coming up with the idea for this book, I told someone my proposed title before even describing its content. I said, "The title of the book is *Beach Money*." And he said, "You mean I can go to the beach and still make money?" I said, "Exactly!" And he said, "I have to read that book!" The title says it all.

You may know nothing about network marketing. You may not even know what it is. But the title of this book got your attention, and that's what caused you to pick it up and start reading. After all, who doesn't want Beach Money?

Beach Money means getting paid over and over again for working one time. Beach Money allows you to go to the beach (or wherever you want to go) and get paid whether you go to work or not. Beach Money does not mean working hard for your money. Beach Money does not mean working smart for your money. Beach Money does not mean working for your money at all. In fact, Beach Money is 100 percent passive income. Passive income is royalty income that comes in week after week, month after month, and year after year.

When you have Beach Money, you have complete and total freedom to live your life the way you want to live it. You get to hang out with your favorite people. When you have Beach Money you can sleep in or take the entire week off. You get to buy whatever you want to buy, whenever you want to buy it. You can live near the ocean, in the forest, in the mountains, or in the desert. Or you may choose to travel the world and explore exotic lands.

It's fun to know that no matter what you are doing, you are getting paid! You are getting paid while you are shopping at the mall. You are getting paid while you are at the movie theater. You are getting paid while you are out to dinner with your family. You are getting paid while golfing. You are getting paid while you are taking a drive through the mountains. You are getting paid while wakeboarding. You are getting paid while you are sleeping! Imagine that each minute a few coins are being deposited into your bank account. I have a close friend who gets paid Beach Money. He was sleeping in front of the TV when his wife came over and woke him up. He said, "Leave me alone, honey, I'm making money!" Let's say you like the idea of Beach Money, but you are not sure if it's for you, because you don't know if you are capable of achieving it. In other words, you really love the idea of getting paid whether you go to work or not, but you don't believe that

"About 5 years ago I had filled my schedule with coaching and consulting clients, and it was then that I realized the only way I could earn the kind of income I wanted to make would be to leverage my time. In the past two years I have leveraged my time through my network marketing business. I cannot think of a better way to leverage! In just two years, I have more than a thousand team members and am earning a six-figure income, which is rapidly growing. Most of my income is generated through the effort of others. I now make more money than I've ever earned before and I have more time for self-care, travel, and volunteer activities."

KATHY PAAUW
Productivity consultant and business coach
Redmond, Washington

it's possible for someone of your background. You obviously won't pursue opportunities that pay you Beach Money, and therefore you will never have it. You will probably be one of the many who spend their entire life working hard at a job or traditional business. And you will spend most of your life "just getting by."

If you're lucky, you will be fine. But if you are like most people, at some point in your life something will happen that completely derails you. For example, you might lose your job or get a big pay cut. Someone close to you may become ill and not have adequate insurance. If you own a business, you might get hit with a big lawsuit or experience a change in the market. These are scenarios we don't like to think about, but we all know that there are times in our lives when we could lose our income, and the bills don't stop. I have watched many friends experience financial ruin because of a drastic unexpected change in their work situation. As you begin to look at the benefits of creating a Beach Money income, you can see that it can help you get through some really tough times, and also give you the resources to live your life exactly the way you choose, without the typical worries of living paycheck to paycheck. There are many ways to create Beach Money. You could purchase rental real estate, buy vending machines, or start a laundromat. You could lend money at a fixed interest rate, become an absentee business owner, or join a network marketing opportunity. The time invested in learning how to create Beach Money will be well worth it, because once you have mastered it, you are financially free for the rest of your life.

For the next few years, you will learn the art of building and growing a business that creates Beach Money. There are tens of thousands of entrepreneurs who have built Beach Money incomes of $5,000, $10,000, $20,000, $50,000, and even $100,000 per month. You may become one of the select few who experience what it is like to be truly free from the struggles associated with linear income. What would your life be like if you had $10,000 per month coming in each month and you didn't have to go to work to get it?

Beach Money sets you free on this earth. There is nothing else like it. I believe you always get what you focus on and put your energy into. For years, I focused on making money in a job and working to increase my income by getting a raise or a better job. My financial growth was sluggish at best. Each year my income would increase by 10 percent or so, until my company downsized or slashed my pay due to budget cuts. Once I started focusing on Beach Money, something miraculous happened. Within a few short years I had a small passive income that began to grow, and grow, and grow! Today my monthly Beach Money income is four times my annual salary at my last job! I focused on aligning myself with opportunities that paid me a passive income rather than a linear income. You always get what you focus on and put energy into.

CHAPTER 2

Get Rich Quick, the Slow Way

You may be like me, and tried to make money at a lot of different things. You may have had a friend ask you to take a look at a business idea involving recruiting other people and you may have been promised that you will get rich. You may have had a relative meet you at a coffee shop and draw out circles on a yellow pad calculating how your income will mushroom into tens of thousands of dollars per month. You may have read in the classified ads about a multi-millionaire who will "build your business for you."

In the end, you probably signed up with a few different companies, listened to their conference calls, and read their training materials. You shared your excitement with friends and family, only to be told, "My neighbor lost his entire savings on a scheme like that," or "Only the people at the top make money in those things." You wanted to believe the promises, but each time you wound up discouraged, with a bunch of upset friends and relatives.

In the 1980s I picked up a book about network marketing at a garage sale for 25 cents. I had no past knowledge of the industry, although the idea of getting paid from the work of others sounded really appealing. Little did I know that the promises of wealth made in that 25 cent book would come full circle and that twenty eight years later I would talk with the author's wife and express my gratitude. That little book gave me the foundation for a journey that ultimately led me to a passive income stream of over $1 million per year. But it was a journey, and it did not happen overnight.

In 1982 I signed up with my first network marketing company, one that offered a nutritional supplement made from algae. I saw a young, fit guy speak to a small audience about the benefits of taking these little green capsules that smelled like fish. He told me about the health benefits of taking the algae. He also explained how someone could lose weight by ingesting four jars of the green sea plants per month. He then showed me step-by-step how I could grow my income into a fortune by sharing these fishy capsules with others. It sounded good to me!

My 22-year-old marketing mind deduced that people reading the *National Enquirer* needed to lose weight. So I got a P.O. box and ran a little $400 ad. I expected my mailbox to be stuffed with $30 checks within a few weeks. Needless to say, my projections were a little off. I received no orders for algae. About four months later, the founder of the company died of old age (he was already in his late seventies) and everything was shut down. I never saw a single check.

But I was hooked. I loved the idea of being able to share a product or service with others and get paid for doing it. I also liked the idea of offering an opportunity to others and getting paid a small cut of what they earned. It all sounded really good.

Next I answered an ad from a company selling 3D cameras through network marketing. I love technology, so this was right up my alley. I went to one of the company's opportunity meetings and got excited. I had no money. The start-up fee was $100 and the camera cost $295. I scraped together every last penny I had to buy the camera. I invited one friend to a meeting. He loved the idea but, like me, he had no money, so he didn't sign up. I spoke with two other friends who said it sounded like a pyramid scheme. After that I was afraid to talk to anyone. I decided to get some advice from my sponsor, and set up a time to drop by his house. I showed up at his front door, which he answered in the nude. His wife and 4-year-old child were also nude. I was not too comfortable with this. He looked like Mick Jagger. I left his doorstep never to return again. The 3D camera business was not for me.

I continued to read about network marketing. I began to learn what to look for in a sponsor and in a company. I started to understand what it took to build a successful team and how to make money. After a few months, I decided to try it again. I met a couple at a business opportunity fair. They were top earners in a small travel company that offered discounted travel packages. I had always been intrigued by travel, so I thought that this one could be really exciting for me. I joined by paying the $100 setup fee and began to invite my friends to the opportunity meetings. I also ran a small classified ad looking for others interested in travel. My

"I have been with my company in Network Marketing since early 2005. After several careers of trading hours for dollars in Corporate Sales, Leading Seminars and being a Psychologist, I finally found this business model. The magic of it for me has been that all I needed to do was what I was taught to do, keep it simple, and teach that to others. Keeping it simple was my biggest lesson! The result is that I have a team that spans the globe, great friends who share my passion, and I am still being paid for work I did in 2005 and every year since then! Leveraged residual income is a different kind of income! As a baby boomer, this business is providing me with a retirement that grows!"

GERI WHALEY
PhD, Network Marketing Professional
Sedona, Arizona

phone started to ring and I invited a few people out to take a look. No one was interested in signing up, but things looked promising so I worked for another two months or so. Then the company shut down! My track record was consistent.

At this point, I decided that I would go the traditional route. I was still in my early twenties and landed a job with a small startup airline doing customer service and training. The airline had an entrepreneurial spirit. It was growing so fast that anyone could create a department and run with it. I started a reservations sales training program, training hundreds of new reservationists each quarter. It was fun and allowed me to be really creative. I learned a lot about people, but my salary was $14,000 per year, and I had a hard time paying my bills.

While with the airline, I uncovered a huge need. Thousands of young people wanted to be flight attendants, but they did not know where or how to get a job in this fiercely competitive airline environment. So I started a little company to train young people to become flight attendants. I did about five 3-hour courses and charged $49 per person. My classes had anywhere from ten to fifty people in them. I started making a little money. But the airline decided that what I was doing was a conflict of interest. I got my first taste of politics and was asked to "cease and desist."

Around this time I was approached by a close friend to join another network marketing company that sold basically everything. The idea seemed like a good one. Instead of buying from the store, I could buy from myself. I could then refer other people to do the same thing. The company had been around for thirty years. It had a track record, a great training program, and a really compelling opportunity presentation. So once again, I joined.

I was told to throw away all my "negative" products and to begin to order from the company instead. I was now set up to buy everything from toilet paper to car wax from my own personal business. By this time, I had spent about $10,000 on start-up fees and products with other network marketing companies and had never made any money. This latest company told me to get on the audiotape-of-the-week and book-of-the-month programs, which cost about $40 per month. I was also ordering about $200 per month in household products. I told my friends and family about my new business. Not one person signed up with me. I was my only customer. I learned to listen to at least one personal development audiotape per week. Each time I got into my car I would pop in a tape. I made sure to read at least one page a day from a positive book. After one full year, I had spent about $5,000 and had no income coming in from my new business.

This pathetic pattern went on for a total of ten years and eleven different network marketing companies. I would get excited and then discouraged, over and over again. I had never sponsored one person or received a check. In fact over the ten years, I probably spent over $30,000 on my "education." I had boxes of products, brochures, audiotapes, books, and seminar flyers piling up in my little bedroom in Tempe, Arizona.

Periodically, I would reread some of the training information and get excited about the promises made by each of these companies. I really had tried. I could not let go of the dream of having a large passive residual income that would give me the freedom to travel, have fun, and play all over the world.

I had proven over and over again, that I was no good at this network marketing stuff. In fact, every time I would join a company, my friends would mock me. I was becoming known for joining companies, getting excited, and quitting. I had a boss who would say, "Jordan, you need to get your head out of the clouds. No one makes money at those things!"

My father hated that I was spending my money with these network marketing companies. He would tell me that I was being scammed and that they are all pyramid schemes. He said that I should focus on getting and keeping a good job. One year at the Thanksgiving table, Dad asked me what I was up to, and I told him about my latest company. This was a big mistake. We ended up in a shouting match. I got up from the table and slammed the front door as I ran out. Happy Thanksgiving!

One time I was visiting my cousin in San Diego, California. Just before dinner, he pulled out a letter that my mother in Chicago had sent to his mother in Las Vegas with quotations from my father saying that I was in a "house of cards." Word was traveling across the country that I was throwing my life away!

So, as you can see, we are probably very much alike. I have had all the nasty experiences that people talk about. I have been patronized, made fun of and ignored by the people closest to me. I have joined companies that have folded and spent thousands of dollars on products that no one else seemed to want. But for some reason, I kept bouncing back.

I NEVER GAVE UP ON MY DREAM

In the summer of 1990 I needed a break. One Saturday morning I took a drive to southern California to go to the beach. I followed the highway signs to the beach cities. As I turned onto Pacific, I caught a brief glimpse of the ocean. I felt a surge of excitement as I quickly found a parking spot on the street.

Two surfers in wetsuits were walking barefoot toward the beach. As I stepped out of my jeep, a pretty girl on a skateboard jumped the curb in front of me on her way to join the other skateboarders on the boardwalk. I could hear music down by the beach. I was about to experience Venice Beach, California, for the first time. The rhythm of drums echoed across the sand. There was a pleasant breeze gently flowing in off the ocean. In the distance, I could see the Santa Monica Pier and the landmark Ferris wheel that has made it famous in many Hollywood movies. The sounds and scents of Venice Beach were familiar. A beautiful woman was playing the harp and singing into a microphone wired to a portable battery-operated amp. A small group had formed around her. A few steps away was a group of street performers encouraging tourists to "come in closer" so they could amaze them with their street acrobatics. As I walked past a few more street vendors, I took in the fragrant scent of burning sage. A few hippies were selling wrapped sage for one dollar, along with tie-dyed T-shirts and bandanas. Bob Marley music was playing on their boom box. The scene was carnival-like. The sun was warm, but the ocean breeze cooled my skin. I was happy and was having fun watching all of the amazing people enjoying themselves on a Saturday afternoon. I approached an outdoor coffee shop next to a juice bar that served fruit shakes and wheatgrass shots. The smell of coffee beans and the beach went well together. A mutt was patiently waiting for its owner to come out of the coffee shop so that they could go play on the boardwalk with the other dogs.

I grabbed a coffee and continued my walk along the beach. It was a perfect day. I loved it. I wanted to be able to do this all the time. I could not help but wonder, "What do these people do for a living?" I assumed that although some were here on vacation, others lived nearby. I noticed that some were just hanging out on the balconies and patios of these million-dollar beachfront homes, just relaxing and watching the tourists walk up and down the boardwalk. What do they do for money? How could they afford to live here? And as I wondered these things, I began to dream about what it would be like to have "Beach Money." What would it be like?

CHAPTER 3

It Rained on My Dreams That Day

I was severely depressed. I was not going to do anything drastic, but I was feeling lost and without purpose. It was a drizzly winter night in Tempe, Arizona. Over the years, I had read every self-help book I could get my hands on and none of them helped. That rainy night I was reflecting on my years of struggle. I could not seem to get ahead financially. Every personal relationship I was in seemed to end in a disappointing breakup. Most of all, I'd had big expectations for my life by the time I hit thirty, and so far I was a complete failure. Nothing seemed to be going right.

I threw on a sweatshirt and stepped out into my backyard. It was overcast, cold, and wet. The ground was soggy. I walked about a hundred yards to the railroad tracks that cut across the back of the property. I started walking along the tracks in the rain, contemplating my life's purpose. This was not a positive environment for getting inspired. The night was misty and gray. A wet, cold wind was blowing in from the west cutting across my path. I walked the tracks for about five miles as the rain came down and the wind swirled between the buildings and homes.

As I listened to my thoughts about why I could not get my life together, I reflected on the self-help books I had read over the years. Many of them suggested that I write down my life dreams in a journal. The most successful authors would say that if you want to create something great in your life, you must first write it down like an architect writes out his plans to build a building. I had read this idea many times over the years, but I had never done it. The authors all said that by putting my dreams in writing, on paper, I would be asking the universe to bring me those things that I desire. They suggested I write my dreams in the present tense, as if they had already happened. But for some reason I had never done that exercise.

After getting home and drying off, I decided I would finally apply some of this advice. The next day I went to the store and bought a journal and a felt-tip pen, and I headed for the airport. I worked for an airline then, and I had flight benefits, so I jumped on a small airplane to the Grand Canyon. I had lived in Arizona for about five years and had never visited the canyon. As I deplaned, I noticed the air was fresh and cool. There were pine trees everywhere. I jumped on a shuttle bus that dropped me off in a small parking lot close to the rim of the canyon. No postcard or photo could capture the beauty of the Grand Canyon.

"When I found Network Marketing, I was a stressed out mom of two (with a baby on the way), and holistic doctor with three clinic locations. When I heard of the possibility of creating a residual income, I thought immediately, "Wow! Now I can have time freedom!" That is what life is all about. The ability and freedom to DECIDE who you want to spend your time with and where you want to be in the world. That is a beautiful and magical thing. Network Marketing has been the ultimate vehicle to give me that freedom. I'm madly in love with the profession and the beautiful life I've been able to build because of it. I get to build beautiful relationships with wonderful people like Jordan Adler and get to build a residual income at the same time. I'm forever grateful for this amazing profession."

DR. DANA MCGRADY
Top Network Marketing Leader and Author
Palm Harbor, Florida

After embracing the breathtaking views, I decided to walk out into the forest. I found a quiet place under an old oak tree that stood about three miles into the woods. I sat on the ground and leaned back against the trunk of the tree. I grabbed my new journal and pen and began to write the story of my life as if it had already happened. I wrote in the present tense, and I wrote vividly and clearly. My descriptions were alive and vibrant. For the next few hours, I set aside all of my doubts, fears, and apprehensions about what was possible. I simply wrote from a place of complete honesty and possibility. My descriptions included the people, places, and things that are important to me. I wrote about my personal life, my business life, my dreams and desires. I described myself physically, mentally, spiritually, and emotionally.

About two hours into my writing, the weather began to change. In Arizona, in the mountains, the weather can change very rapidly. The wind began to blow and the temperature dropped about twenty degrees. All of a sudden some heavy gray cumulus clouds formed over the top of the mountain where I sat and the temperature dropped another ten degrees. I realized that I should probably begin my journey back because I sensed that it might start raining. I was right. Within a few seconds, it started to rain. The rain was cold and the wind continued to blow.

I did my best to hold my journal close to my body to keep it dry, but the pages got soggy. I walked quickly back toward the edge of the canyon as the temperature dropped to about thirty-five degrees. The rain turned into sleet just as I entered the Bright Angel Lodge. I opened my journal. Some of the ink had run down the damp pages.

The warmth from the fire burning in the huge fireplace across the room was inviting and filled the room. I sat down on some colorful cushions next to the fire and continued to write the story of my life. For the next few hours, I lost myself in my future life, but as I wrote it, I began to live it in my mind as if it had already happened. Later I would realize that this was the most important moment on the whole journey.

I got back on the plane and headed for Phoenix. Just as the self-help gurus suggested, I placed my journal next to my bed on my night stand, which was two cinder blocks and a piece of wood. Every night for the next year I would read one or two pages from it. Each time I read, I got more and more excited. I anxiously awaited my new life.

A year had gone by, and nothing from my journal had come true. Not one thing. I felt duped! Once again, I had failed. What was wrong with me? I took that little journal and threw it in a box in my closet and forgot about it.

Seven years later...I smile at my girlfriend as we continue to unload my new cabin furniture into the living room of my dream home in the forest. My new home is a beautiful log-sided mountain retreat with a huge wraparound deck and cathedral ceilings. It backs up to national forest land, and I have pine trees growing up through the wooden decks. The air is fresh and clean. When a breeze blows, the trees sound just like the ocean. The air is so clean that when you breathe it almost hurts your lungs! At night, the Milky Way looks like a streak of smoke cutting across the sky. It's pure heaven.

As I am opening boxes, I notice a journal on top of a pile of books. It was the journal that I had written at the Grand Canyon seven years earlier. I opened the journal, read the first two pages, and started to cry. Everything in this journal had come true in my life. I now had the home of my dreams. I was driving the car of my dreams. I was physically fit and happy. I had an amazing girlfriend who has become my lifetime friend, and I had a passive residual Beach Money income of over $30,000 per month that allowed me to travel the beaches of the world. I had found my dream life. I really don't know why this works. I am not a psychologist or metaphysicist. But I do know that if you grab a pen and notebook and find a quiet, inspiring place where you can write for a few hours, you can do the exact same thing that I did and continue to do each year of my life. Consider writing the story of your future life in the present tense, as if it has already happened. Set aside all your fears, doubts, and apprehensions about what's possible, and just write as if you were a child again, dreaming from your heart. Write until you have your entire life exactly how you want it. Then read one or two pages a night for about a year and then throw it in a box.

CHAPTER 4

"You'll Never Make
Any Money at That!"

We've all heard those skeptical, grating, low-energy, whiny comments made by cynics who have never done anything with their lives. And each time we hear about a new opportunity, echoes of these comments make us hesitate to take determined action. I believe that much of my fumbling through my first eleven companies was due to a subtle but nagging fear or doubt. Nothing great has ever been accomplished in a state of hesitation.

Hang gliding provides a great metaphor to demonstrate this. Imagine having doubt or hesitation while launching off a mountain. The result can be quite devastating. In fact, one time I watched a hang glider pilot decide not to launch after he had already committed to his run off the mountain. In those critical few seconds, while he was running off the mountain, he questioned the launch conditions. He abruptly stopped, and slipped and fell over the edge of the steep launch ramp. He tumbled into the rocks and fortunately was only slightly injured. Hesitation can cause any business to stall. It's tough to attract customers when you are doubtful about your enterprise. Hesitation is a poor state to be in if you are trying to lead a company, attract people, or raise money. Even mediocre businesses can become wildly successful if the leadership team has an unwavering belief in its crusade. Committed leaders can quickly and easily attract other leaders. Teams grow fast in a fearless state. In fact, when a leadership team carries out its mission with sincere and determined action, the laws of logic seem to evaporate into thin air. This is how individuals and companies do the impossible. Most great success stories are unrealistic tales that come true because a group of people believed in the impossible and fearlessly shared their dreams with others.

When we join a company and begin working, if we have any lingering concerns about our product, industry, or personal skills, our results will be mediocre at best. In most cases we will fall flat on our faces. Lingering doubts stemming from our past experiences and conversations with others will destroy any chances we have for success.

"You'll never make any money at that."

"I can't believe you paid money to get into that!"

"Only the people at the top make money in those things!"

"Why don't you just get a real job?"

"Those things are all scams!"

"Sounds like one of those pyramids!"

"That's nothing but a house of cards!"

Comments like these, playing over and over again in our head, will create doubt, fear, and hesitation. When these self-sabotaging statements begin to take over, any chance for success is gone. Caution sets in. Our focus is directed inward. We become paralyzed by fear and we will do whatever is necessary to protect ourselves from pain. Unless we can shift this energy, it's over.

In my tenth year in business, I experienced a realignment that set me up for success. My point of view shifted. I was beginning to work as a distributor in my twelfth company, and had invited five people to hear a speaker at one of the company's introductory business meetings. Two people showed up. I brought them to the front of the room and we sat in the front row. (I have read that "You'll Never Make Any Money at That!" people who sit in the front row make the most money. I sit in the front row at everything I go to, including seminars, meetings, concerts, and opportunity presentations. When the meeting ended, I introduced my two guests to the speaker, who was the number one earner in the company, making about $60,000 a month. Although I had never met him, I introduced my guests to him as if we knew each other.

A couple of weeks later, I attended a tour event that had all five of the top earners speaking on stage. Once again I sat in the front row, and at the end of the event took my guests to meet each of the speakers. I acted as if they were five of my closest friends. I continued doing this for about six months. My team started to grow. I was at an event in San Francisco and once again, all the top earners were there. By this time they knew my face and my name. Something happened that evening that broke things loose for me.

My consistent attendance in the front row and my insistence on introducing my guests to the speakers gave me some notoriety. I was invited by one of the top earners to join him and the others for dinner after the meeting. I was just starting out, earning less than $200 per month. At dinner, I found myself sitting with a group of people who were all earning between $10,000 and $60,000 per month. I learned from the conversations taking place that night. As I listened, it occurred to me that these people were just like me! They told stories of defeat that made mine look silly. Some of them had been financially broke more than once in their lives. One of them had tried many businesses prior to having any success at all. They were friendly and personable. They even gave me their home phone numbers! They shared stories that inspired me. Jay Smith, one of the most well-respected leaders in the company, handed me a personal note of encouragement during dinner.

I read the note. It said, "Nothing would make me happier than to see you get your executive promotion!" I couldn't believe it! Jay noticed me! I started to feel like they were becoming my friends. Most of all, I really began to believe I could do it.

Beginning the very next day, I approached my business with a renewed level of conviction and confidence. The doubt was completely gone. I wanted to be a top earner. I wanted to be on the inside circle. I wanted to travel and walk on the white sand beaches of the world. And now, I finally knew I could do it. From that day forward, I was a leader and I began to attract other leaders. Whenever I had a setback, I would get on the phone with one of my new friends and get some encouragement. I would remember that night and envision what it would be like to travel with this group and possibly share the stage with them someday. That kept me working and excited about my Beach Money future.

"The first time I saw Jordan speak I was at a Network Marketing Mastermind event in Dallas, TX. I was 20 years old and I sat with my mother in the front row taking notes. Jordan was one of the first people to inspire me to grow a big business. Today I speak in front of thousands and lead a team of over 300,000 people. Thank you Jordan for paving the way!"

SARAH ROBBINS
#1 Money Earner and Global Leader
Best Selling Author
Troy, Michigan

CHAPTER 5

Jordan Is Short!

At my first company convention, I watched the top earners walk across the stage. I remember sitting in the crowd and thinking to myself, I'm supposed to be up there! Most people leave these conventions excited and motivated. I left this convention anxious and unsettled. But it was exactly what I needed to get motivated. I decided that I would never again be sitting in the audience at a convention. I vowed to be on stage with my team, getting recognized for huge accomplishments and changing lives. Two years later, my business had really taken off. I received a phone call from Melanie at our company headquarters asking if I wanted to speak at our next company convention. I had never spoken in front of a large group in my life! My vision of being on stage with the other top earners was coming true, and I was terrified. Six years earlier, at a previous job, I saw a posting for a corporate trainer position. I thought it sounded like a great job as long as I didn't have to speak in front of groups! I applied for the job and got it!

I was so afraid to speak that on the day I was to train my first class, as I was driving to work, I prayed I would have an accident so I wouldn't have to face the class. I have read that public speaking is number one on the list of things people fear the most. Death is number two. I was almost ready to die so that I wouldn't have to speak that day.

Well, I didn't have an accident and I didn't die. When I arrived at work, my boss pushed me into the room full of students and I got through it. I think I did fairly well. But up until the day I was asked to speak at the convention, the largest group I had spoken to was about forty people. I was now being asked to speak for three minutes to a group of 14,000 people! For the next two months I had many sleepless nights. I rewrote my three-minute speech many times. I rehearsed each version over and over. I had fears of freezing up. What if I forgot my speech in front of all of those people?

Finally it was convention time. I was up front, in the crowd taking in the excitement of the day. High-energy music played loudly, and many enthusiastic distributors were clapping and dancing to the music videos on the big screens mounted on the walls. We were all asked to be seated and the event was under way. About two hours into the production, I felt a tap on the shoulder. It was time for me to go backstage. As I slipped behind the giant curtains, I noticed thick wires running in every direction. The sound system boomed out front and the crowd roared with excitement and anticipation. The top earners were all backstage congratulating each other and encouraging me. I was blind with nervousness. My greatest dream and my greatest fear were about to converge. I was told to come up the steps leading to the back of the stage.

I heard the announcer say, "Ladies and gentleman, from Tempe, Arizona, Mr. Jordan Adler!" The crowd roared and sprang to its feet! I was showered with appreciation. Loud music played as I walked onto the stage. Looking through the bright lights at the thousands of people in the stadium, I was overtaken with emotion. As I walked to the front of the stage, my knees became weak. To keep my balance, I grabbed the top of the podium and in that moment I realized that it was about one foot too high. The top of the podium came to the bottom of my nose. I looked up at the huge video screens and the only thing I could see was my nose and my eyes! But suddenly the podium started to lower. It was on hydraulics! As it began to shrink, the audience started to laugh. They might as well have flashed a huge sign on the screens announcing: "Jordan is short!"

At that moment I completely lost my train of thought and forgot my speech! My biggest nightmare had come true! But it all turned out just fine. The crowd got a good laugh. I had a chance to be on stage with the top earners, and most of all it was an experience of a lifetime. That was the beginning of a rich career in training and speaking. I have since had the opportunity to train and speak all over the world to hundreds of audiences and tens of thousands of people. I still get a little nervous, but have learned to use that energy and turn it into excitement.

The rewards that come with speaking to groups have been indescribable. Some of my most fulfilling experiences in personal development have been in front of a crowd of people. Public speaking is a skill that can take you to new heights in your career. I recommend that you start public speaking right away. If you are like me and have some fears, simply start small and grow into it.

CHAPTER 6

The Numbers Don't Lie

As I mentioned earlier, after ten years and eleven companies, I had nothing to show for my time, energy, and money but boxes of training manuals and some old, stale, expired nutritional products. I had given up on the network marketing industry forever.

And then I met Russ. Russ was a young multimillionaire in the network marketing industry. He was married with one child, and lived in a multimillion dollar home in Scottsdale, Arizona. He was driving a sports car and had made megabucks in the industry at a young age. We never went into business together, but I was intrigued by his massive success. We met through a mutual friend at a café, and he invited me to his home to visit his home office and learn some of his secrets. I was told to look for a giant fountain framed by tall palm trees. I pulled into his circle drive. I had never been inside a home like this one. The oversized entryway was framed by four large white pillars. I was with my friend Dale. We rang the doorbell. The door was big and it appeared heavy. It opened slowly. Russ was dressed in Bermuda shorts and a Hawaiian shirt. His home must have been 10,000 square feet. The next thirty minutes changed my life forever.

He brought us to his home office, which was lined with many framed photos of his family standing on beaches in many parts of the world. There were tall bookshelves filled with hundreds of personal development books. It was a hot summer day and Russ offered us a cold glass of water.

We started off talking about Russ's family, but the conversation soon turned to business. I told Russ my story. I needed to know how Russ did in five years what most others failed to accomplish in an entire lifetime. He said, "In the business of recruiting, you'll need to be prepared to recruit twenty to thirty people. It doesn't matter if you are in real estate, financial planning, insurance, or network marketing. You must recruit twenty to thirty people to start with." He then said, "One third of your recruits will do absolutely nothing. One third will do a little. And one third will make a good income. Usually, one of them will build a group of thousands."

He told me that he had seen many people unsuccessfully try and change these numbers. He watched as many newcomers tried to motivate their slower-moving distributors by holding workshops and trainings. He said, "In the end, some will do it and some won't. All the energy and time you put into trying to get your weaker team members to grow is time wasted. You are better off using that time to help your motivated distributors and to recruit a few new people to get started in the business."

To prove his point, he challenged me to find a successful real estate broker and ask him or her how many recruits it takes to find one big hitter. "In almost all cases," he said, "the answer will be twenty to thirty." He then challenged me to join a good company and go out and recruit twenty to thirty people. He said that I would never have to work again! This was a little tough to believe, but I trusted him and was definitely willing to give it a try. I don't know if what he said was actually true. But I do know that I believed him at the time, because he possessed the lifestyle that I wanted.

I had never in my life recruited anyone for anything. But I knew that if I would consistently meet with three or four people per week, I could certainly sponsor one per month. A two-year plan sponsoring one person per month would give me somewhere between the necessary twenty and thirty people.

So I joined my twelfth network marketing company. I was still working a job in management at the airline and had a staff of six trainers working for me. I had very little time to build a side business, except for my lunchtime.

My new network marketing company distributed telecommunications services like long-distance, pagers, and Internet service through a network of independent distributors. I became an independent distributor for this company. To build a successful income, I needed to find twenty long-distance customers and then sponsor others to do the same. As my distributor organization

"Several years ago I was asked a question by someone who introduced me to network marketing: 'For $100,000 would you jump out of an airplane without a parachute?' Quick to respond, of course, my answer was 'No!' He said, 'Too bad, you missed out on $100,000. Did I tell you the airplane was sitting on the ground?' For years nobody told me that airplane was on the ground so I always stayed away from jumping into network marketing. My friend helped me to understand and I jumped! Consistent effort can make anyone a six-figure income in this career if they are willing to jump! How do I know? Because it happened to me and I have watched many others leap, survive the jump, and make more money than they ever dreamed of!"

DEMARR ZIMMERMAN
Marketing consultant
Salt Lake City, Utah

grew, I got paid for the training of my team and the usage of the telecom service. In network marketing, you get paid for the volume of business brought into the company by you and your team each month.

I formulated my plan. I would use three lunches per week to show my business plan to potential recruits and customers. I would learn a very simple, twenty-minute, one-page opportunity presentation, and I would schedule three appointments per week at the Coffee Plantation, a café near my office on Mill Avenue in Tempe. My goal was to show my business to three people per week (twelve per month) and recruit about one person per month for twentyfour months. This would put me in the range of twenty to thirty recruits and I would never have to work again, according to Russ!

I recall reading an article in *Time* magazine about a crazy guy named Marshall Applewhite. Marshall and his girlfriend, Bonnie Nettles, led the Heaven's Gate religious group. The group's end coincided with the appearance of the Hale-Bopp comet in 1997. Applewhite convinced thirty-eight of his followers to commit suicide so that their souls could take a ride on a spaceship that they believed was hiding behind the comet carrying Jesus. Don't you think that if this crazy guy could recruit thirty-eight people to commit suicide and jump onto a comet with Jesus, you might be able to find twenty to thirty people to do network marketing with your company?

About the time I met Russ, I was living in a 1950s block-construction three-bedroom rental home with two roommates and a dog. My portion of the rent was $200 per month. I was driving a 1987 Jeep Wrangler with a smashed front end. My possessions consisted of only a small professional wardrobe, the jeep, a $700 hang glider, a bed, and an end table made of two cinder blocks and a piece of plywood. My annual income at the time was under $20,000. Each month was a struggle to pay my bills. During this time, I had never used a computer or owned a cell phone.

Month after month I would do a balancing act to avoid having overdraft charges at the bank for bounced checks. I had a philosophy: my goal was to make sure that the amount of the checks I had written never exceeded the amount that was in my account at that time. This was a really good theory. If I could figure out a way to earn more than I spent, I would be in good shape. To this day, I have never balanced a checkbook. So month after month, I would have multiple overdrafts due to my rough miscalculations. In fact, there were many months when I received three to twelve overdrafts on checks that had bounced. One time I went to the bank and the teller took my bank card and wouldn't return it.

I needed a way to track my progress. I drew a three-foot-wide by four-foot-high grid on my bedroom wall and subdivided it into one hundred squares. The top promotional position in my company was executive director (ED) and I needed to sign up twenty customers to qualify for all the income. I also read that if I could complete one hundred opportunity presentations, I would be on my way to financial freedom. So I wrote "ED" at the bottom of the grid as my goal. At the top of the grid I wrote "Find 20" to signify acquiring my twenty customers. With my current situation, I was pretty stressed out, so I wrote "Have Fun" at the top of the grid as a reminder not to take things too seriously.

I held my lunchtime business meetings on Tuesdays, Wednesdays, and Thursdays. After each lunch, I would write the date in one of the squares on the grid. My plan was to fill the grid and become an executive before the grid was full. Each week I could see at a glance if I had done my three presentations. If I missed a few I held myself accountable to make them up the next week. This is what the grid looked like.

Have Fun   **Find 20**

9/21	9/21	9/23	9/25	9/26	9/27	9/27	10/1	10/2	10/5
10/6	10/6	10/10							

ED

At the time I was building my business, I was single and actively dating. If I met a woman I liked, I would ask her out on a date and invite her back to my apartment. We would do a little tour of the house and when we would get to the bedroom she would notice the grid on the wall over the bed, with the phrases "Have

Fun!" and "Find 20." You can guess what she imagined. And she would ask, "Who's ED?" This was not easy to explain!

Well, as I filled the grid, my business started to grow. I would average about one new recruit per month. Some months I would recruit one, some months two, and some months none, but I focused on sponsoring one new distributor per month. I also looked for opportunities to have meetings for others on my team. In the beginning, I was often the only one willing to do any work, so it was usually just me.

I would set up appointments with people I knew. I would show them my business plans to see if they were interested at all. About one in eleven would want to sign up with me, usually a few weeks after our initial appointment. It took a lot of patience, because there was very little money to be made in the early stages of my business growth. At the end of each appointment, I would give the person some literature to read, and I would follow up a few days later. I learned to have faith that everything would work out just the way it was supposed to. I wasn't working lots of hours at my business, but giving up my lunches for two years with no guarantees was a test of my belief in myself and my opportunity.

After twenty-four months, I fell just short of my goal to personally sponsor and train twenty to thirty new distributors—I had nineteen. But something great began to happen. Jackie, my sixteenth recruit, discussed our opportunity with her friend Judy. Judy was a mother, a student, and a secretary. She told me that she would never speak in front of a group but she was really excited about our program. She began to build a team from the living room of her home in Albuquerque, and in a matter of a few months she had about fifteen personal recruits. Her team began to grow. And it grew. And grew. And my checks grew. And grew! Within two years she had over 12,000 people on her team and my income skyrocketed!

I had never experienced anything like this. The money came in whether I worked or not. But my checks were small and never exceeded $200 in a month for my first eight months. During my first two years, my income was a healthy part-time income. In my twenty-fourth month in the business, my income was about $2,800. I then experienced something that I had heard and read about called momentum. My checks rapidly began to grow. By the end of my thirty-third month, I was making over $34,000 per month! I was making twice as much money per month as I used to make per year at my job!

This was my income growth over my first three years in the business:

1992	
Sept.	(less than $100)
Oct.	(less than $100)
Nov.	(less than $100)
Dec.	(less than $100)

1993	
Jan.	(less than $100)
Feb.	(less than $100)
March	$180
April	$470
May	$850
June	$980
July	$1,167
Aug.	$960
Sept.	$1,130
Oct.	$720
Nov.	$1,060
Dec.	$1,470

1994	
Jan.	$1,540
Feb.	$810
March	$1,570

1994 (cont.)	
April	$4,680
May	$3,100
June	$2,180
July	$3,930
Aug.	$2,950 (2 years)
Sept.	$1,350 (everyone told me it was saturated)
Oct.	$3,410
Nov.	$2,340
Dec.	$3,500

1995	
Jan.	$3,780
Feb.	$5,900 (2-1/2 years)
March	$6,230
April	$8,500 (I'm glad I didn't listen)
May	$13,655 (the largest checks I had ever seen)
June	$15,070
July	$18,505
Aug.	$16,700
Sept.	$20,915 (first time I ever danced to the bank)
Oct.	$21,550
Nov.	$34,750

As my income grew, I began to pay off my $36,000 in credit card debt. I got caught up on all my bills; I bought a home in the pine forest of Arizona, purchased my first luxury convertible automobile, and bought a cell phone!

My dreams were coming true. I was being asked to speak at conventions. People wanted my autograph at events. This was really hard to understand. Just a few months earlier, I was buying macaroni and cheese at 33 cents a box to keep my food expenses down!

I began flying around the country in our company owner's private Gulfstream jet and staying in luxury five-star resorts across the country. I finally had more money in my account than I needed to spend. My checks were finally clearing. This was a great feeling. Russ was right. I needed to recruit about twenty to thirty people to find my builders. And once I found them, I had a passive income that came in whether I went to work or not!

In my fifteenth month in the business, I realized that I was going to make a career of it, so I resigned from my airline job. I was a middle management trainer with a small staff. When I told my boss my plans, he seriously questioned my sanity and tried to convince me that I was making a bad decision, but I reassured him I was making the right choice.

At the airline, when a top-level executive left, a notice announcing the departure was posted on bulletin boards. But I was not a top-level executive, so my departure was not announced. I thought it might be fun to create my own announcement. I took one of the departing executive's announcements and altered it to say, "Notice: Senior Trainer Jordan Adler retires to pursue other opportunities." I posted the notice in the employee lounges, break rooms, and work spaces. My boss took some heat and had to remove them himself. He was not amused. What was he going to do? Fire me? When my income hit $20,000 per month, he decided to join me and became a full-time network marketer with us!

I built this business in the old days before the advent of the Internet. I did not even own a computer at the time. Today we have tools and technology that can accelerate the growth of any business, but the fundamentals of business building have not changed. I speak from experience. It would be easy for young, high-tech entrepreneurs to say that the old-school fundamentals used to work, but that today a higher-tech model is needed for fast growth and retention. Don't get me wrong. Technology is important and can streamline the process of growing and managing an organization. But the fundamentals of building relationships do not change.

In the past three years, I have broken records in a technology-based network marketing company using the fundamental principles of business development. With over 2,000 active distributors, I became the number one money earner without using any Internet strategies. I built my business from scratch, one person at a time. I have personally sponsored 122 people in 145 weeks and built a team of 20,000 distributors in less than 3 years. My income has grown from a few hundred dollars per month to over $100,000 per month with a consistent residual check that exceeds $50,000 per month.

I did no advertising or purchasing of leads. I did no e-mail auto-responders or mass marketing. I was not given a downline or paid to come over to my new company. I am proud that I started the same way as any other new distributor.

I cannot take full credit for this growth. I have attracted many great leaders into my organization. Most of them had little or no network marketing background. I can say that they all have a strong entrepreneurial drive. I see many young entrepreneurs struggle with the fundamentals of growth in a network marketing company. Their biggest problem is leaning too heavily on the Internet and technology to build the business. Many will completely abandon the basic principles for growth and trade them in for automatic systems designed to scoop people up in mass quantities. They expect the technology to do the work for them. Inevitably they are baffled by how to attract a group of loyal entrepreneurs and keep them for the long haul.

Here are some points to consider:

1. You must have a plan and stick to it for eighteen to twenty-four months.
2. You can build serious income on a lunchtime schedule.
3. Usually your big income growth will be tied to the work of one or two people.
4. To find the one or two, you must sponsor and train at least twenty to thirty people.
5. Sixty to 90 percent of the people you show your opportunity to will probably be uninterested.
6. Technology will not replace the fundamentals of building a successful business.
7. Regardless of how financially tough your situation is, you can turn it around in eighteen to twenty-four months with a consistent plan.

CHAPTER 7

How to Get Paid Big Money Whether You Go to Work or Not

L ast week I worked five hours and got paid about $20,000. I haven't decided yet if I will work next week or not. I may decide to take the week off and take a trip to Las Vegas with my girlfriend. Either way, I will receive about $20,000 in income all over again next week. It's a nice feeling of security, knowing that money comes in whether I work or not. Some weeks I don't work at all and my income goes up.

True financial wealth is created through leverage. Leverage is a simple concept to understand and an easy one to implement as long as you have the right systems in place. Actually, with leverage, making a lot of money is easier than working for your money. When you work hard for your money, it's all about what you do. When you have leverage, it's very little about what you do and everything about what you start.

Let's refer to the income that you receive from your own work as linear income. Let's refer to the income you receive from the work of others as nonlinear income. With linear income, you work once and get paid only once. In other words, if you stop working, you stop getting paid. With nonlinear income, you get paid over and over again for working once. In other words, your efforts accrue. The work you do today pays you over and over again. You get paid long into the future. So as you continue to grow, the income you made this month is stacked on top of the income you made last month. And the income you make next month is stacked on top of the income you made this month. So over time, you can accumulate an income stream that will eventually equal your bills. Once your bills are covered by your passive nonlinear income stream, you are financially free. You now have Beach Money! You can now go to the beach and not have one single worry about your monthly bills. Everything is covered by your passive income stream, whether you go to work or not!

Unfortunately, the idea of leverage is not taught in school or in the workplace. Therefore, it's foreign to most people. In my classes at the University of Illinois, I was never taught about leverage. I was taught how to write a résumé and basic interviewing techniques. But no one I know has ever become wealthy by writing a good résumé and doing a good interview.

When applied correctly, leverage can completely transform your life. Imagine what your life would be like if you had money pouring into your account each month that had little or nothing to do with your efforts. Does this sound too good to be true? Most people immediately write the idea off as some type of scam or money game. Actually, almost all great fortunes have been created through leverage.

Here is a great example of leverage. Let's say you want to go from San Diego to New York City in the winter. You decide to travel by moped. You plan to take your trip in January. You give yourself an entire month for the ride. How does this sound? It wouldn't be much fun. You would need to make lots of stops. You would be very, very cold. You would need to contend with snow and ice and wear lots of clothing to prevent frostbite. You just might end up in the hospital. Our bodies were just not meant for long cross-country rides on a moped.

Or, you could travel in style on a high-performance Gulfstream jet. You would arrive in New York City in a few hours relaxed and refreshed. The jet provides a much more comfortable experience. The flight crew handles everything and in a few hours you barely notice the wheels touching down on the runway in New York. By leveraging money and technology, you arrive in New York more quickly, more safely, and more comfortably.

You are on a trip to achieve Beach Money. A nine-to-five job is the worst vehicle in the marketplace today for achieving financial freedom. It gives you no significant leverage. Jobs aren't bad. They pay the bills. But they happen to be extremely poor vehicles for the trip you want to take. Trying to go from San Diego to New York on a moped is like trying to get to a Beach Money lifestyle in a job that pays you desk money.

By making the transition from your traditional business or job to one that provides nonlinear income, by making the decision now to focus on opportunities that pay you over and over again for working one time, you will be well on your way to your Beach Money lifestyle.

CHAPTER 8

My Hourly Pay Went Up When I Started Working Less!

For years, I would check out the job postings on the bulletin board in the break room at work. I was a supervisor and the thought of getting promoted to manager meant more responsibility, recognition, and even a little more pay. I might have a staff someday and get to do performance reviews and job interviews! Typically I would scan the board for something that paid between three and five dollars more per hour than I was currently making. That meant an extra $500 to $700 per month in income before taxes. It would cover my car payment or help me pay my credit card bills.

I read books and attended classes on how to write a good résumé and how to do a dazzling interview. I knew all the right moves: use the interviewer's name, and shake hands with a firm but not bone-breaking grip. Have a clean, crisp, and conservative résumé. Dress for success, which included an ironed shirt and polished shoes. I wanted to be sure the interviewer felt appreciated by me so I sent a thank-you card immediately after an interview. Most people don't send thank-you cards. I learned that the art of "kissing up" (as pathetic as it sounds) worked fairly well.

Year after year I got raises and gradually grew from a mere $8 per hour to a stunning $15 per hour! And then it happened. The airline I was working for cut my pay from $28,000 per year to $14,000 a year after filing for bankruptcy. I had a choice. I could quit my job or take the pay cut. I chose the pay cut. I was so grateful to upper management for allowing me to stay on. I wasn't paid much, but they really appreciated me and isn't that what really matters?

In the traditional job model, in order to increase your hourly pay, you must ask for a raise or find a better-paying job. If you are on a salary, you are more likely to work more hours than you are getting paid for and thus your hourly pay goes down.

As I was developing the idea for this book, I realized that Beach Money allows you to work less and get paid more per hour. Unlike the traditional model that pays you for your time, with Beach Money you get to benefit from what you start, not what you do. And if you cut back on your hours, your hourly pay actually goes up. Here's an example:

"As a professional singer and actress in New York City, I didn't have a way to create a residual income in my life. I was always cognizant of the fact that I got very well paid for what I did when I was in a show, but I wasn't necessarily building anything towards my future. When I was presented with this opportunity to share a product that I loved with others and get PAID to do it over and over as it grew, I moved forward with focus, enthusiasm, and a desire to help and support others. Now every day, I get to actively look for ways to celebrate and uplift people... and I get to help others do this as well. It has allowed me to grow in every aspect: as an entrepreneur, coach, mentor, speaker and writer, with the ability to affect others positively on a deeper level than I'd ever experienced as a performer. It's like a magical show that never ends!"

JULES PRICE
Professional Singer and Network Marketer
Sarasota, Florida

If I'm making $5,000 per month working 200 hours, I'm earning $25 per hour. In the traditional model, if I work fewer hours, my monthly pay goes down. But in my Beach Money model, let's say I cut back to 100 hours per month. I still get my $5,000. I'm now making $50 per hour. What if I only worked 50 hours? I make $100 per hour. I have a friend who makes about $1,000 per hour in our business. She works less than one hour per month and consistently gets a check each month for $1,100! Beach Money income gives you a chance to work less and increase your hourly pay!

This idea really excited me, because I had always believed that the only way to increase my hourly pay was to get my employer to pay me more money per hour or to get a new job!

So, let's say you have created a passive Beach Money income of $2,000 per month and you work for ten hours that month. Your hourly pay that month is $200 per hour. What if you only work five hours that month? Your hourly pay goes up to $400 per hour! Now that's leverage. Is this for real? Absolutely! I have hundreds of friends with Beach Money income making $5,000 to over $100,000 per month and the less they work, the higher their hourly pay!

When people ask if I work in my business full-time, I have a hard time answering because the question only applies in the traditional job world. In the world of Beach Money, there is no full-time or part-time; a ten-hour work week can pay you five times more money than a full-time job. You can be on a part-time schedule and make multitudes more than most full-time employees as you grow your business.

CHAPTER 9

A Few Ways to Make Money

Let's take a look at some of the typical ways to increase income and compare them to my Beach Money model:

It's clear from this comparison that the Beach Money model is by far one of the best choices for creating unlimited growth potential and time freedom with little to no up-front investment.

Get a Second, or Better Job	Beach Money
Boss decides pay increase	No boss (you decide pay increase)
Limited income potential	Unlimited income potential
Linear income (paid once for work)	Nonlinear income (get paid over and over for working once)
Stop working–stop getting paid	Stop working–still getting paid
Quit–stop getting paid	Quit–still get paid
Just a job (minimal personal growth)	Personal development opportunities

Go Back to College	Beach Money
You pay up to $200,000 tuition	You pay less than $1,000 to get started
Guarantee–a diploma	Guarantee–get paid while you learn
No income during college	Graduate in one to four years with Beach Money income
Classroom training	On-the-job real-life business training

Open a Franchise	Beach Money
Hire and manage employees	No employees to manage or pay
Buy capital equipment	No capital investment
Invest $50,000 to $200,000 up front	Invest less than $1,000 up front
Limited potential–up to $75,000 per year after the third year	Unlimited potential–up to $1,000,000 in the first three years
Franchise fees	No franchise fees
Long-term leases	Work from home
Three to five years to break even	Make back your investment and start getting paid right away
Your business owns you	Total time freedom–work when you want to

"Simply stated - network marketing has given me the three P's!! Purpose, Passion, and a Paycheck! There is no other industry that would allow me the freedom to stay at home with my kids while building a lucrative global business. Purpose: is waking up every morning excited about my day and whose life I get to change in some positive way. Passion: this profession challenges, intrigues, and motivates me to be my personal best while teaching others to do the same. Paycheck: There is nothing like residual income. Getting paid over and over for the work that you do once. I have been to more places with my family in the last few years than I have in my lifetime because of this industry."

MELISSA BARLOCK
Work-From-Home Mom
Burlington, Ontario Canada

CHAPTER 10

How a Minor Shift in My Thinking Transformed My Bank Account

People often ask me, "How do you accomplish so much in so little time?" I've learned that even the most complicated things can usually be broken down into three easy steps. That single lesson made my life infinitely more manageable and expanded my bank deposits beyond my wildest dreams. In fact, my Beach Money lifestyle kicked in when I began breaking down my projects, goals, and dreams into three easy steps. A Beach Money lifestyle is a few months away for you, too, if you will apply this simple concept.

Some people say it's easier said than done, but I say it's easy to say and easy to do. The biggest challenge is stripping away all the extra stuff we add to make ourselves feel important and smart! Here are a few examples:

If you are learning to fly an airplane, you'll need to learn to do three things:

1. Take off
2. Fly
3. Land

Once you have mastered these three things, you can fly safely and successfully.

If you are an architect, you need to learn to do three things:

1. Assess clients' needs
2. Create designs
3. Communicate specs so designs can be built

That's it. When you've become really great at these three things, you will have become a masterful architect!

Of course, there is always more you could learn about being a pilot or an architect. Simplifying the steps involved makes achieving your dreams, goals, projects, or tasks manageable, which lowers your stress level and makes you much more productive.

I'd like to share a story about two guys, Jason and Roger. Both of them would like to lose weight and get in shape. Jason is well-educated and prides himself on his ability to do extensive research and absorb a lot of information. Roger is more practical by nature and usually looks for the quickest path to success.

Jason decides to learn everything he can about losing weight and getting fit. For the next three months, Jason checks out every book he can find on health and fitness at the library. He registers for a class at the community college and even buys the *Encyclopedia of Health* at the local bookstore. For at least an hour a night, Jason reads, highlights, and takes notes as if he were studying for a law degree.

Roger understands the principle of leverage and is results-driven. He writes down three basic steps for getting fit:

1. Sweat every day
2. Stretch every day
3. Eat 70 percent natural, unprocessed, and unpackaged food (fruits and vegetables) every day

After three months, who do you think has lost the most weight? Who is most fit? Obviously, Roger. Who knows more about health and fitness? Probably Jason, but his results stink. Is this starting to make sense?

Remember, duplication and leverage are keys to a huge Beach

Money income and a Beach Money lifestyle. Anything hard to figure out or implement will slow down or stop duplication and leverage. Keeping it simple is critical. I like to do the "8-year-old test": if an 8-year-old can't do it or explain it, I don't do it either.

A REAL-LIFE THREE-STEP PLAN IN ACTION

Someone once asked me to write down three things that I wanted to accomplish in the next three months and post the list where I would see it every day. I made my list and looked at it daily, even though I was not sure how I would actually achieve my three goals. But after three months I had accomplished all three. Here's the game plan for getting what you want in record time:

Step One

Write down three things you want to buy or do in the next three months (this is the most important step).

EXAMPLES:

- Register your kids in a private school.
- Go back to school yourself.
- Make some repairs on your home (things that have been bugging you!).
- Buy front-row seats to a concert or play that you have always wanted to see.
- Hire a housekeeper.
- Donate $500 to your church or to a family in need.
- Drive up the California coast and stay in seaside lodges along the way.
- Take a hot-air balloon ride.
- Take a weekend getaway in the woods.

- Take a trip to Las Vegas.
- Rent a condo on the beach.
- Open a college fund for your kids.
- Upgrade the sound system in your car.
- Buy a swing set for the kids.
- Attend a four-day Tony Robbins event.
- Buy a second car.
- Put a down payment on a house.
- Buy a new bedroom set.
- Buy some new appliances.
- Take a three-day vacation at the beach.

Ground rules:

1. Your three goals have to get you really excited.
2. You must be able to do or schedule each item on your list within three months.
3. Don't be practical; you have permission to splurge.
4. Limit the list to just three items. You may have four or five goals you really want to accomplish, but pick your top three for now. After you've accomplished those first three, you can add three more to the list.

Here's something to consider as you undertake this exercise: Answer this question: Do dogs like bones? Most people would say, "Yes, dogs do like bones." But if I place a steak and a bone on the ground and let the dog choose, which is he more likely to go for? He would probably go for the steak! Dogs don't like bones. Dogs settle for bones, but they salivate over steaks. As you make your list, go for the steak.

One training seminar I attended suggested that your dreams don't really count until they're on your calendar. In the past, I had hopes and dreams that dragged on for years. I talked about taking a cruise to the Virgin Islands for 15 years! Then I did something very simple: I put it on my calendar. Three months later, I was on the cruise and enjoying one of the best weeks of my life!

Step Two

What actions will you take right away to begin to move you toward these things you will be getting in the next three months? Limit your actions to three things. What three things can you do in the next three months to move you toward accomplishing your three dreams?

1.

2.

3.

Step Three

Expect and allow the universe to provide you with all the resources you need to attain the three things you have written down. This is not a "To Do" step. It's a "Releasing" step. It's a "Letting Go" step. Simply do steps one and two, and then let go of the outcome. Expect good things to happen.

My Beach Money lifestyle comes from breaking down my projects and goals into three simple steps. I just do this over and over. I teach three simple steps. I keep it so simple that an 8-year-old can do it and teach it. You will love this, because for the first time in your life, everything will become so simple and doable.

CHAPTER 11

Bed Wetting and What It Means

Your mind is a powerful computer. It controls how you feel, and how you feel determines what you attract. Your mind does not know the difference between what is real and what is not. Your imagination can create and your imagination can destroy. Usually when something is not going exactly the way you want it to, you have created a scenario in your mind that is taking power away from what you say you want. That power is taken away through the bad feelings created by your thoughts. Regardless of whether your thoughts are based on reality or not, your feelings are real and your feelings determine what you attract.

Let me explain in a story. This is quite personal, but I feel the need to share all the details with you, as embarrassing as they may seem.

I crawled into bed after a full day of training at the airline. It was a cool night and the heat was blowing through the vent coming from the ceiling. My studio was small, with old dingy carpeting. It smelled of lingering cigarette smoke left over from the last renter. I curled up and fell asleep knowing that the alarm would go off at 5:30 a.m. This would give me exactly enough time in the morning to shower, dress, and prepare for my 8 a.m. class.

Sometime in the middle of the night, I woke up lying in a puddle of warm liquid centered right under the midsection of my body. It was quite uncomfortable. I quickly got up, stripped the sheets and headed for the laundry room. I threw them into the washer. I stepped back into my studio apartment and fell asleep on the couch.

The next morning I headed off to work to teach my class. After work I went home, prepared dinner, and fell asleep. At about 2 a.m., I awoke to a warm puddle of liquid under my midsection once again. This time I was feeling a little sick. I stripped the sheets, threw them into the washer, and slept on the couch. I was very run down and tired the next day at class. I found myself feeling lightheaded throughout the day and even imagined spending the next fifty years of my life wearing an adult version of diapers. A few of my students told me that I looked sick. Every half-hour I had the urge to urinate, so I ran to the bathroom to relieve myself as quickly as possible.

I called the doctor, described my embarrassing problem, and scheduled an appointment. That night I tossed and turned. I struggled to fall asleep. At about three o'clock I woke up to the same shameful set of circumstances. As I rolled over, I realized that I had a pinhole leak in my waterbed! Rejoice! I didn't need to wear diapers for the rest of my life!

You are probably wondering why I had to tell you this story. I want you to know that your mind does not know the difference between what is real and what is not.

When faced with a set of circumstances, your personal human computer creates scenarios to attempt to explain them. Your body then responds to your brain's interpretation. I had evidence that something unusual was going on in my bed. My brain created the following interpretation:

1. I had an accident.
2. There is something wrong with me.
3. I am sick.

4. I don't feel well.
5. I may be sick for the rest of my life.

I was interpreting my set of circumstances as some serious problem with my health. My actions were driven by my feelings of being sick. I made an appointment with the doctor.

How does all of this apply to your life and your business? Your mind is an intricate computer that takes in a bunch of data and then makes deductions from the data. These deductions guide you in one direction or the other based on your feelings about them. How you feel about a set of circumstances based on what you say about them can drastically alter your life's course.

Here's an example: Your neighbor and your cousin both get involved in network marketing. Neither of them makes any money and both of them quit.

Possible interpretations:
1. No one makes money in network marketing.
2. Network marketing does not work and only the people at the top make money.
3. They got in too late.
4. They didn't receive good training.
5. They are lazy and don't make money at anything that they do.
6. They quit too soon.

You can see that if you choose interpretation 1, 2, or 3, you would probably be turned off by a career in network marketing and never pursue it again. Based on your determination, you would say that network marketing is not a very good business model and you would avoid it in the future. You would also be cutting off any future opportunities to create a Beach Money lifestyle for yourself and for your family!

If you had chosen interpretation 4, 5, or 6, you might believe that there is still hope for you with some good training, motivation, and consistency. You could possibly still feel great about network marketing as a profession and create many reasons to continue to pursue your dreams. As a result, you may end up with a passive Beach Money income of $20,000, $30,000, or more per month. The circumstances did not change at all. Your interpretation of them did, and it led you down a completely different path.

Let's look at another example:

1. You meet a charismatic person. He has made millions in network marketing over the past six years.
2. You go to a network marketing seminar and hear ten people speak about the fantastic lifestyles they have created for themselves over the past few years.

Possible interpretations:
1. They all got lucky.
2. They are all trying to sell me something.
3. They all got in at the top.
4. I could learn a lot from them.
5. They want to teach ambitious people like me how to be successful.
6. They were once just like me, and they have grown into great leaders.

Again, depending on which interpretation you choose, you will feel a certain way. Your feelings will guide your actions. Can you see that choosing interpretation 1, 2, or 3 will result in a different future than choosing interpretation 4, 5, or 6?

Take a look at your circumstances and ask yourself how you are interpreting them. How do you feel about how you are interpreting them?

Early in my network marketing career, I began to interpret things in a way that made me feel really good about the industry and my potential to build a large passive income. I created a great story about what it would be like when I had Beach Money. My good feelings guided me to the opportunities and the people that helped me to see my dreams come true. So don't underestimate the power of your mind and how it can lead you to your ultimate dream.

If you have an area of your life that you continue to struggle with, take a look at how you are interpreting it and how you are feeling about your circumstances. Take a look at what you can do to shift your interpretation to create a more powerful context for yourself and your life.

CHAPTER 12

A New Perspective

An emotionally charged event can completely alter our view of life. As our views shift, our lives shift. We begin to look at things from a whole new perspective. Our decision making is altered. We make different choices. We base many of our decisions and choices on our perspective. So as our perspective shifts, so do our decisions and choices. I have identified a few events that have occurred in my life that have completely shifted my view of life.

My shift in perspective has caused me to make different choices around business and finances. These experiences have shaped who I am today. Have you noticed that one event, one meeting, one dream, one introduction, one experience can completely alter the direction of your life? Here are some events that ultimately led me to my Beach Money life.

A LOOK INTO YOUR FUTURE

I used to own a 1987 Jeep Wrangler. It was really beat up. The air conditioner didn't work. Neither did the windshield wipers. The rag top had been stolen at a local swap meet. Arizona summers can get as hot as 115 degrees, and the monsoons can bring torrential downpours. This was not a fun jeep to drive in the summer or in the rain.

One evening during rush hour I was about two miles from home when a 17-year-old in a beat-up old Chevy Impala pulled out into traffic. I T-boned her car going about thirty-five miles per hour. Fortunately, no one was seriously injured, but the front end of my jeep was smashed in. We called the police and exchanged phone numbers. At about nine o'clock that night I was driving down highway US 60 going about seventy miles per hour when the hood of my jeep began to shake. With a violent crashing sound, the hood flew up and slammed into my windshield, shattering it into a spiderweb pattern of cracks. The latches had been damaged in the earlier accident and were not holding it down securely. I had moving traffic all around me and could not see a thing. I stopped in the middle of the freeway and slowly worked my way over to the shoulder. After catching my breath, I secured the hood with some rope and continued on my way.

The next morning on my way to work I saw a police car in my rearview mirror. It appeared that he was squinting as he tried to look through the cracks in my front window. He probably figured if he couldn't see through it, I couldn't either! He pulled me over and wrote me a ticket. I had insurance but could not afford to pay the $75 deductible to replace the glass. Paying the ticket was out of the question, given my current state of affairs.

On my way home that evening, I was caught in a heavy rainstorm. It felt dangerous to drive my Jeep under these conditions with the shattered windshield. Although my view was obstructed by the cracks, I could see the road as long as I focused beyond the windshield toward the horizon. In fact, with some squinting, the cracks would blur out to a point where they almost didn't exist.

In that moment, I realized that in my pursuit of business success I tended to get distracted by the challenges, problems, and inconveniences along the way. When I focused on them, they became bigger and more distracting, just like the cracks in my windshield. The challenges would repeatedly prevent me from seeing where I was going and accomplishing my goals. I would work so hard trying to fix the problems that my business would suffer. For example, I had money problems. Checks were bouncing. I would get so focused on my problems that I would not focus on the fundamental activities important to building a successful business. I realized that I always get what I focus on. I could no longer afford to focus on my current challenging circumstances. To achieve my dreams, I needed to keep my eye on creating my future. And when things got tough, I needed to remember to focus my attention on my ultimate destination, the road ahead.

YOUR LUCKY BREAK

As a small boy, I had learned about the "Adler curse," which stated that anything that could go wrong in a situation would go

"Network marketing gives us options, which to us means freedom. We believe we are unemployable. Having set hours and answering to another did not fit our personalities. We enjoy the freedom to create how we want to help others choose what they want in their lives. We love all of the options network marketing gives us; the freedom to do what we want, when we want to do it, and in the style we like!"

BOB AND BETTY ANN GOLDEN
Automotive industry and real estate
Las Vegas, Nevada

wrong for an Adler. Well, I was an Adler, and therefore everything that could go wrong would go wrong for me! I know this sounds ridiculous. As children, we take on labels and adopt them as absolute truth. These labels become our identity. Somewhere along the line, I had adopted the identity of being unlucky. We all have these labels and they can shape our life experience in a profound way. When we adopt a label, we send out hidden messages for people to communicate with us in a way that is consistent with our identity. Labels such as funny, happy, depressed, animated, successful, energetic, open-minded, and creative can all shape the future of a young child. Whether we were given the label by a parent or friend or whether we came up with it ourselves really does not matter. Our personalities are shaped by our identities. For most of my young life I had a curse of bad luck following me! My label was unlucky. My identity was, "I am an unlucky person!"

Every business I started failed because of the curse. My relationships didn't work out because of the curse. People took advantage of me because of the curse. I got injured because of the curse. There was no escaping it!

Have you ever noticed that some people have all the luck? They win at almost everything they do? They seem to get all of the breaks. Other people seem to be unlucky all the time. They can't get anything right. They get in more auto accidents, have more illness, can't keep a job or a friend, and they are always being taken advantage of. It appears that life has handed them a raw deal.

I never came out on top. I was a loser. Nothing ever seemed to go right in my life. Any time I had a success, I would look for the downside. Anything good was inconsistent with my identity, so I expected something to always go wrong, and usually it did.

My college degree was in landscape architecture. Early in my working career, I had a job as a draftsman. I spent eight to ten hours a day at a drafting board designing landscapes. The owners of the company I worked for were very successful, well-respected landscape architects. We had a mutual respect for one another, and I really enjoyed working with them. One day, one of the owners came over to me, watched me draw for about a minute, put his hand on my shoulder, and said, "You have a star following you." The words I heard were, "You have a LUCKY star following you." I had never experienced the feeling of being lucky. It felt great. I wanted to be a lucky person.

For whatever reason, in that moment, I became a lucky person. And what happens to lucky people? They get all the luck! And, guess what? I began to get all the luck! My luck changed over-night. Miracles started to happen in my life. Every day something lucky would happen to me. I started getting promoted rapidly. My income began to rise. I started meeting all the right people. I became a magnet for good things.

This may sound like hocus-pocus, but here's my explanation. When you see yourself as unlucky (or whatever other negative word you use to describe yourself), your subconscious mind begins to look for and find evidence that supports that belief. We all want to be right. I'm not a psychologist, but I do know that we attract what we think about! If you identify yourself as successful and really believe it, you'll begin to attract success. If you see yourself as fun, you'll be-gin to attract fun! Your subconscious mind will actually draw to you all that is consistent with whom you know yourself to be!

When my boss told me I had a star following me, I could see and feel that star. At a gut level, I believed him. At that moment, my life changed forever. For the next few years, I went on to attract all the lucky breaks. My last opportunity was the luckiest find of my business life. Today I enjoy being the number one money earner in a company doing millions per month in business. So if you want to begin to attract all the luck, simply declare yourself as a lucky person and begin to believe it! Take on the label of someone who has all the luck! Then start to look for your lucky moments all week long. You will be surprised by how much luck you attract into your life on a daily basis.

A SMALL ACT THAT WILL CHANGE YOUR LIFE

In 1981 I moved into a dingy studio apartment in Tempe, Arizona, on the corner of University and Hardy. It smelled. I paid $238 per month and that included utilities. My next-door neighbor was a 58-year-old overweight man named Don. Don's wife had left him. His kids had not spoken to him for over eight years. He was extremely lonely and depressed. Don's life was a mess. Every night he would drink and tell me of his troubles. His breath smelled of cigarettes and liquor.

Don inspired me. For the past twenty-five years I have thought of Don at least once a month. He wrenched me to my core. I made a sincere commitment never to let myself be like Don. I needed to read, learn, and grow so that I would not end up like him. He inspired me to create a life of abundance. I began to read and attend seminars. I started running and taking care of my health. I went on to take risks and pursue opportunities.

Don has no idea that his inspiration created a ripple effect and set into motion a chain of events that ultimately led to my positively impacting the lives of thousands. Don saw his life as a mess with no purpose. He was almost on the verge of suicide. I had compassion for him. And he helped make me who I am today. I guess I saw my alternative future in Don. A few bad choices and I could just as easily have been him in twenty or thirty years. In a strange way, Don inspired me to take positive action.

You may not want to live Don's life any more than I did, so you can begin to see the connection that you have to all other human beings around you. Imagine that each time you meet someone new, give someone an encouraging word, send a positive greeting card, make a phone call, or have a short conversation you are firing off a chain of events that can impact the lives of thousands of people over time. People make choices based on how they feel in that moment. Your words and actions impact the choices others make in their lives. Think about a single decision you made, maybe ten years ago, that completely altered the course of your life.

Envision the most important person in your life today. How is your life different today because you met that person? How did you meet? What would your life be like if you had not met that person? Now ask yourself what single event could have occurred years ago that may have prevented you from meeting that person. How important was that one event? One small act, the act of moving in next to Don, set off a chain of events that changed my life and the lives of thousands of others.

YOU DON'T NEED TO KNOW EVERYTHING

When I was learning to hang glide, I spent hours and hours, weekend after weekend learning to launch and land, over and over again. I would stumble up a little training hill over cactus and rocks until I was bumped and bruised. I would come home with grit and dust in my teeth and a bad sunburn. I did this for months. During my training, I also practiced small left and right turns. I would climb up the hill with an eighty-pound glider strapped on my back. The wind would nearly blow me over. Sometimes it would take thirty sweaty minutes of fighting the glider to get to the top of the hill, all the while trying not to fall into a jumping cholla cactus. It was hot and grueling. Many weekends I wondered why I was putting myself through this.

Finally, after logging hours of launches, landings, and turns, and reading about rotors, thermals, power lines, barbed-wire fences, squall lines, cloud suck, and glass-offs, it was time to take my first mountain flight. Here's the problem: you can't learn how to fly until you fly. There are just too many unanswered questions. In fact, trying to know all the answers before flying will mess with your head. At some point you just need to go fly!

The fundamentals can get you through anything. In fact, trying to learn everything there is to know about flying a hang glider will screw you up. You'll get paralyzed with fear, because your brain can't retain all of it! Running off a mountain with Dacron and aluminum strapped to your back is not the most logical or sane thing to do. I ran off because I wanted to fly! That's why I was willing to go through all of the agonizing training and injuries. I wanted to feel the wind in my face. I wanted to experience the world from above. I wanted to hang from the sky. I wanted to know what it was like to be a cloud! I wanted to feel what it was like to be a bird! I regularly get questions and calls from aspiring business builders wanting to know how to become successful. They routinely ask, "Where do I find people to talk to? What should I say?" In other words, they want to know how to go about it. But learning everything you need to know before doing it will tie your brain into little knots. It's just not possible to fully prepare yourself for what's to come. Just like flying a hang glider, sometimes there is no logical or sane reason to do it other than that you have a dream that needs to be played out in your life. Learn the fundamentals and then just go! Run off the mountain. Have faith that you will know what you need to know when you need to know it. You'll learn how to feel your way through it and you'll blow yourself away when you begin to fly.

Take time to master the fundamentals and then just go! Don't wait to have all your questions answered. They will never all be answered. If you wait for them all to be answered, you'll never do what you need to do to create the positive results you are looking for. Just go.

YOUR GREATEST GIFT

In grade school I was the kid that got picked last for every sports team. In fact, the only reason I got picked at all was because everyone had to be on a team. Otherwise I would not have played at all. No one wanted me. It angered me and made me resent the other kids in the school. It cut like a knife. At times I felt really isolated and alone. This was one of the most difficult times in my life, and it shaped my beliefs about myself. I wasn't very good in sports and so I didn't have much value to the others as a team member.

Hidden deep within this experience was a blessing that I could have never predicted. Today, I build my own teams, and everyone gets to be on my team! In fact, I am one of the top team builders in the world! I get to pick who is on the team! I offer an opportunity to anyone wanting to play. Those experiences from my childhood provided me with the ambition to create and lead great teams that span the globe.

Sometimes the most difficult experiences in your life can bring you the greatest gifts. And sometimes the gifts don't reveal themselves for years. Be grateful for your trials.

"I have been a full-time network marketer for 12 years. I work from home, don't have a boss, no set hours per week, and I can run my business from anywhere with my laptop or smart phone. My incomes comes in automatically every month and my check has had a comma in for over 10 years. I was able to retire from my 25 year counseling career because of this business. I have been able to learn things and do things that I previously did not dream were possible for me - build a big team, speak from the stage, and write three books about our profession, put on retreats for women to help them be more self confident and successful."

JUDY O'HIGGINS
Former Women's Counselor
Cottonwood, Arizona

CHAPTER 13

The Day Momentum Hit

After years of getting in and out of network marketing companies, I decided I would give it one more shot. I signed up with my twelfth company in ten years and heard about an opportunity meeting. I was told I could bring guests. I had five confirmed guests. I showed up for the meeting about an hour early. The company leaders had told me over and over again that if I wanted my guests to be at the meeting, I should pick them up. They also said that if I asked my guests to meet me at the event, there was almost a 100 percent chance they would not show up. I have since learned that this is true.

The meeting was scheduled to start at 7:30 in the evening. At 6:30 I was the only one there. I had told my guests to meet me at 6:45, and at 7:15 I was still waiting for them. One of my guests finally showed up at 7:20. We sat in the back of the room. Groups of people started arriving and lining up at the door. The room vibrated with conversation and energy. Everyone seemed to be excited. There was lots of talk about the charismatic speaker who knew how to make money. I felt the excitement in the room build as the crowd's energy grew to a feverish pitch. At 7:30, the crowd became silent and then jumped to its feet and roared with applause as the famous Al Thomas was introduced.

I felt distressed. Al was so good. He was fun. He was funny. He knew how to make money. And here I was sitting with my one single guest while Al had a room full of over 200 people! How did he do it? I had worked so hard to invite five people and only one had showed up. I decided once again that I would never make it in this business. I thought to myself, "I could never be as good as Al!" About thirty minutes into the meeting, Al had a few of the people in the front row stand up. He introduced them as his guests. In that moment, I realized that Al had only three guests at the meeting. Al did not have 200 people at the meeting. Al had just three. I had one person. The distributor next to me had no one with her. A distributor named Sandy had two guests. David had one guest and Kari had invited ten guests but no one showed up to meet her. The room was filled with about 150 distributors.

Some of them had a few guests and many had none. I then began to understand the magic of momentum.

THE MAGIC OF MOMENTUM

What is momentum and what does it feel like? When does momentum begin? Can momentum be created, or does it just happen? How much luck is involved? I had heard about the big leaders who had 1,000, 2,000, and even 5,000 people joining their teams every month. It seemed almost surreal. How could they attract such large groups of people? Were they doing mass recruiting? Were they using some secret system that they weren't telling us about to grow such big teams so quickly? Did they work long hours to generate this kind of supernatural growth? Were they using an elaborate Internet-based recruiting approach?

There has always been a big mystery around how this much growth could happen for some people and not for others. In this chapter, I will solve the mystery of momentum and unveil the secrets of creating momentum. You will know exactly what momentum is, how it feels, and how to create it. You will begin to redefine momentum in a way that will make it real for you. Momentum is a buzzword that is thrown around this profession. But it's not what it seems.

I don't know when momentum started for me. It might have started when I signed up my first "business builder," or when I decided to be a leader, or the day that ten people joined my team, or when my monthly check exceeded $10,000 for the first time. Or it may have happened when I was recognized for having a monthly pay increase of $3,000, or when my annual income exceeded $1 million.

I learned something the night I heard Al speak in Scottsdale, Arizona. I learned that Al only had three guests at the meeting. But Al's team had a total of about thirty guests. Not one person had more than three guests. If half of Al's guests signed up that night, his team would add about fifteen new distributors. And Al had meetings like this going on all across the country. He was only at one of the meetings, but leaders on his team were conducting similar meetings in Chicago, Los Angeles, Columbus, Miami, Des Moines, and Sacramento on the same night. If fifteen new distributors joined Al's team in each of the six additional cities, that would add an additional ninety new distributors to Al's team.

By the way, Al also had 150 distributors in other cities across the country who did not make it to the meeting that night, but they did meet with some of their friends at their homes. Twenty-six of those 150 distributors also signed up new distributors. Al's team signed up 131 distributors that night. How many did Al sign up? Al signed up just one. Over the course of a month, he would do two or three of these meetings per week, but he had hundreds of these meetings going on around the country. He would have over 2,000 new distributors join his team each month, but he would only bring in three to five each month himself. Al never brought in lots of people on his own. In fact, I learned that no one ever brought in lots of people. However, lots of people each bringing in a few every month appears as momentum.

Imagine having a group of 20,000 people on your team. If just 10 percent of them bring in one person a month, you will have added 2,000 new distributors to your team. That's momentum. It will produce some very large five and six-figure monthly checks! If you are unable to envision having 20,000 distributors in your group, then maybe you need to hear this story. I had never successfully built a group of even two people. I was sitting at the basketball stadium in Phoenix watching the Phoenix Suns play the Dallas Mavericks. For a few seconds, I imagined sitting in the stadium all by myself. There were about 20,000 empty seats in the stadium. I could never imagine building a team large enough to fill all 20,000 seats, but I could definitely fill the seat to my left and the seat to my right! What if I were to do just that? I then wondered if the three of us could fill the ten seats immediately surrounding the seats we were sitting in. That sounded reasonable. Now I have ten people sitting in my little group, but the entire stadium is still completely empty. How could ten of us even think of filling a stadium of 20,000 seats? I wondered if our little group of ten could get one or two people each and thereby grow our section to thirty people. Of course that was possible! Doesn't it then make sense that we could grow our thirty distributors to one hundred new distributors? Could one hundred of us each invite a few and eventually fill five hundred seats? Of course! Can you begin to see how five hundred full seats could turn to 1,000 and then eventually 5,000? How long would it take us to fill 20,000 seats if we started with 5,000?

I have been around the networking profession for years and I have never seen any one person build a large team on his or her own. I have seen many people find a few people and over time turn that group into thousands. When thousands of people each set out to find one or two people each month that can create substantial growth and income!

TIMELINES AND GROWTH

The amount of time it takes someone to bring another person onto the team does not speed up as the team grows. As more and more people join a team, it just appears that growth speeds up. If I have one person on my team and it takes that person two weeks to bring another on board, then growth appears to be rather slow. Let's assume that eighteen months from now, I have 1,000 people on my team, and fifty of them show the business to a potential partner that month. Each prospect takes two weeks on average to join. Over the course of the month, fifty new people join my team. That's nearly two people per day, but I did very little actual work myself. Although the time it takes for someone to come into the business (two weeks) has not changed, the sheer numbers make it feel like the growth is speeding up.

THE APPEARANCE OF MOMENTUM IN NATURE

A seed turns into a plant, a plant turns into a stand, and a stand turns into a forest. This all happens as a result of cell division, and the more cells there are, the faster the rate of growth! The cells don't divide faster and faster. There are just more of them, so more cells are dividing in a shorter period of time! In the beginning there are fewer cells, so there are fewer cells dividing. In the beginning there are fewer plants, so there are fewer plants dividing.

A human being starts with a cell. A family starts with a couple. A community starts with a few families. The baby boom was an example of lots of families making babies all during the same twenty-year period. Was the boom caused by momentum? Or was momentum caused by lots of individual families having one or two babies each? Have you ever noticed how fast children grow once they hit a certain age? As they grow, they have more cells dividing and therefore they seem to grow even faster!

Think about how the common cold spreads. It starts with a few people getting sick. It appears that people are getting sicker faster as the cold spreads, but in actuality there are just more people spreading the cold to others.

AN EXAMPLE OF WHAT MOMENTUM LOOKS LIKE IN A NETWORKING BUSINESS

- **Month 1:** You bring in one to five people.
- **Month 2:** You bring in one to five people. No one does anything. You've spent $1,000 and have earned $300.
- **Month 3:** You bring in one to five people. One person brings in one and then doesn't do anything more. You earn about $100.
- **Month 4:** You bring in one to five people. Your group adds three distributors for the month and you get your first promotion. You earn another $200 but you have spent another $500.
- **Month 5:** You bring in one to five people. Your group adds ten distributors and you get your second promotion. You earn about $500 but you've spent another $500.

- **Month 6:** You bring in one to five people. Your group adds another ten distributors and this is your first profitable month. You earn about $700 and spend about $200. You are tired and overworked and have lost money overall. You want to quit. You question whether it's worth it. Your friends and family ridicule you for working so hard for so little.
- **Month 7:** You bring in one to five people. Your group is now adding three people per week. You're not sure if this will work. This is the most critical time; 95 percent quit here.
- **Month 8:** You bring in one to five people. Your group starts adding one distributor per day and you make $1,500.
- **Month 9:** You bring in one to five people. Your group starts adding two distributors per day and you make $2,500.
- **Month 10:** You bring in one to five people. Your group starts adding three distributors per day and you make $4,000.
- **Month 11:** You bring in one to five people. Your group starts adding six distributors per day and you make $6,500.
- **Month 12:** You bring in one to five people. Your group starts adding ten people per day and you make over $10,000.

You have now cracked the code of momentum. You now know what momentum feels like. You understand the dynamics of the system. You have positioned yourself to earn $30,000 to $50,000 per month within two to three years. You start to get excited about your Beach Money future.

You will never meet 99 percent of the people coming into your organization. They don't live in your city. Your business begins to take on a life of its own. Your group adds 200 to 500 new distributors per month. Your residuals grow each month. You have 4,000 distributors in your entire group. You are a hero in your company. People want to know your secret. You are asked to speak at the company convention, although you have never done anything like this before. People want your autograph. You start thinking about writing your first book.

"Who would have imagined that someone that did not go to college would be traveling the world making 6 figures in her first 6 months. Network marketing has changed my life and I love the ability to help others. I know if I can do it, you can do it too."

KAREN AYCOCK
Work-from-Home Mother of Four
Dallas, Texas

CHAPTER 14

Rolodex Marketing
(Money Does Grow on Trees!)

In the 1980s I read a book by Harvey Mackay called *Swim with the Sharks Without Being Eaten Alive*. It's a work of genius. In it Harvey writes, "You can predict the future of someone's income by looking at the size of his or her Rolodex." Have you ever noticed that the people with the most success are also the most well-connected people you will ever meet? Most successful people can get anything done with a quick phone call, because they know someone. They have a large Rolodex and they have relationships with the people in their Rolodex. Here's an outrageous example: If you wanted to get something done quickly, and you needed to pull a team together, who would be better equipped to help you, Elon Musk or the guy who works at the local convenience store? Not to minimize the value of a store attendant, but which one has the larger network? Which one has the resources to help you pull your team together quickly?

Let's say you are looking for a job. Who would you call? If you had a big Rolodex with lots of quality contacts, you could probably get a job by making a few phone calls. And you would probably get the best results by calling the people who also have the largest Rolodexes. You might hear, "Let me make a few phone calls and I'll see what I can do." It's almost like a tree of relationships. Money does grow on trees! Connected people know other connected people. Strong networks run deep. When you invest your time to become well connected, you begin to attract others with connections. Within about two years, you can set yourself up to never want for anything again in business. At your fingertips, you will have all you need to get anything done. Your network will become your most valuable resource.

As I write this, I realize that people under the age of 30 probably don't know what a Rolodex is! There is a difference between a Rolex and a Rolodex. But it's not a bad idea to get to know the people with big Rolexes, because they probably have big Rolodexes as well!

Your electronic contact manager is simply a modern-day Rolodex. Your contact manager holds your network. A contact manager containing 500 contacts is worth millions of dollars to you if you manage it effectively. The network that I began back in the 1980s has grown into the thousands. My contact manager is the most important business tool I have. It's the key to my success.

Your success will be largely determined by:

1. The number of contacts in your contact manager.
2. The quality of your relationships with the people in your contact manager.

Here are some tips and ideas for growing your network and building your relationships using your electronic contact manager: You have probably heard the saying, "It's not what you know, it's who you know!" Actually it's not just who you know, it's who knows you! You want to make sure that the people in your network know you and know what you do. This is as important as you getting to know them. You want them to think of you when they are ready to do business. In other words, are you in front of them enough for them to remember you when the time is right for them to do business with you?

I had a conversation with someone who was struggling in his business. I asked him how many people he had in his contact manager. He told me he had 450 people. I then asked, "How many of those people know exactly the nature of your business and what services you provide?" He said only twelve people knew what he was up to! You cannot be successful if the people in your network don't even know what you are up to!

Let's go over a few important things you can do to maximize the use of your personal electronic Rolodex:

1. **Add one or two people to your contact manager every day (one per day is 365 per year).** Set this as a goal. Your job is simply to meet them. You are not trying to sell them anything. As time goes on, you will get to know them and also look for ways to help them.

2. **View your contact manager as an opportunity to "give back."** Scan your contact manager each day and ask, "What can I do for someone in my network today that will add value to their life?" Look at your contact manager not as a resource for getting, but as a resource for giving. Each day, do something positive for at least one member of your network: Give a referral. Make a phone call just to check in. Send a thank-you card. Send a "thinking of you" card. Send an "I would like to get together with you" card. Congratulate someone in your network. Make an introduction to another member of your network. Host a networking lunch and invite a bunch of people from your contact manager (you can invite them with a call and with a card). Throw a party just for fun. Schedule a short coffee meeting just to get to know a member of your network and find out how you can help him or her.

3. **Cold calling is not necessary.** Your network can connect you with all of the resources you need to be successful. When you meet someone new, your objective is to get to know them so that you can become a great resource to them. Add them to your contact manager. You will also educate them as to what a good referral would be for you by showing them what you do in business. As a result, you will have many people who will want to go into business with you.

4. **Make notes in the "Notes" section of your contact manager.** Keep a log of people's interests and the dates and topics of past conversations you have had with them. Your contact manager does just what its name says. It allows you to manage your contacts. Your contact manager is a tool that assists you in creating lifelong associations with the people you meet.

Ask yourself the following questions about the people in your network. This will give you an idea of what you'll need to do to advance the quality of your relationships with them.

1. Do they know you? Do they know what you do? Do they know what you look like and what you are interested in? People will only do business with the people that they remember when they are ready to take action. If you don't come to mind when the time is right, you will not get the business. They must positively associate you with the service you provide.

2. Do they trust you? Would they call you for advice or ideas? Do they consider you a valuable resource? People typically

will only do business with people they trust. By positioning yourself as a trustworthy advisor/expert, you are much more likely to get phone calls from potential business partners and customers.

3. Do they consider you a friend? Do they like you? People love to do business with friends. Make each person in your contact manager a friend and do things with them that friends do together.

4. Can they depend on you? Are you rock-solid in their eyes? Do they know that you will be there for them if they need you? Be consistent and dependable. Call people back when they call you. Do what you say you are going to do. Follow through with your commitments.

Most people who get into a business view each person they meet as a potential sale. If the person does not sign up or buy, they are forgotten forever. Successful business owners know that their lifelong association with someone is far bigger than the sale. They know that some people will result in multiple sales over their lifetime and others may never buy anything at all. Some people may refer lots of people to you and others may just become close friends. Some people may go into business with you today and others may never join you.

So to recap, by focusing on these five things, you can maximize the value you'll get from your electronic contact manager:

1. Add people to your network each day and put them into your contact manager.

2. Get to know the people in your network.

3. Make sure the people in your network know you and what you do.

4. Acknowledge the members of your network with phone calls, cards, and e-mails.

5. View your network as an opportunity to "give" versus an opportunity to "get."

Most people today do a terrible job of acknowledging and connecting with the members of their network on a regular basis. You can differentiate yourself in the eyes of everyone you meet by doing these five simple things. Although they each take a few minutes per day, you can optimize the business in your company and on your team if you take the time to do these things.

I can hear some of you saying, "I already do this. I put people into an automatic e-mail campaign to make sure they hear from me on a regular basis." I believe that e-mail campaigns are a big mistake if you want to build a successful business. Blanket e-mails annoy people and most of them end up in spam folders. You cannot automate the personal touch. You must take the time to connect with the people in your network. You will accomplish more in a five-minute personal phone call to one person than you can by blasting out 2,000 e-mails to everyone on your list.

In his book, *The Harvey Mackay Rolodex Network Builder*, Harvey Mackay writes, "If I were being mugged and had to choose whether to hand over my wallet or my Rolodex file, it would be no contest. Losing my wallet is inconvenient, scary, expensive, and a pain in the back pocket. But losing my Rolodex file would be devastating. I can replace all my credit cards and I can live without a few dollars. But the information I've gathered over the years—now that's irreplaceable.

"How do you do it? Like many great ideas, it's very simple. When you meet someone new, make a note of when, where, and how you met and anything interesting you learned about that person, such as hobbies, family data, special interests, and so on. As soon as you get back to your office (and by this I mean the same day), make a Rolodex card or entry in your contact management system and file it immediately. You should also note any follow-up contact, a thank-you card or an article sent out, and when your next contact will occur. That way you can make sure your Rolodex file is working actively for you and not just sitting dormant. If you don't have a specific reason to contact someone, you might still make a note to follow up in three to six months. Later when you get that reminder, you'll find a reason to be in touch. If you have a genuine desire to stay in contact, it's easy."

CHAPTER 15

You Will Doubt!

I attended a great workshop hosted by Dan Sullivan, the creator of the Strategic Coach in Chicago out by O'Hare Airport. Dan opened by talking about the current economic outlook and how some of the greatest opportunities occur during tough economic times.

Many people are feeling the pressure of a volatile and unstable economy. We live in a time of economic uncertainty. In other words, many people have lost confidence and are feeling the pressure of an unknown future.

During times like these, many people become paralyzed and fearful. Just months ago, you couldn't lose money in the stock market even if you tried. Today there is so much volatility that one day you can have hope and the next you feel completely deflated. So now, people have lost confidence. Confidence is at an all time low. Dan suggested that confidence is not a function of how big someone's bank account is; confidence is a feeling. The challenge of leadership is to find confidence and hope during times of trouble. I would like to propose that, when you offer hope for a better future, you can restore confidence and instill that confidence in others.

In my last company, the number one earner used to say that, regardless of where you are financially, there will be times when you lose confidence and you will doubt.

As an entrepreneur you will doubt when you start making $1000 a month. And when you hit $10,000 a month, you will question whether you can ever make $20,000. When you hit $20,000 a month, you will doubt if you could ever make $50,000. Even at $50,000, you wonder whether $1 million per year is possible. And when you hit a million, you'll probably doubt if you can keep it.

We are doubting humans. That is just what we do. Actually, no matter where you find yourself, there may be times that you will doubt. You may lose faith that it's possible for you to ever get there. So what's the solution?

According to Dan, you must first gain your own personal confidence back. Then you must learn to instill confidence in others. What does this look like?

Well, many people are looking for the security of knowing that things will get better. As you regain your confidence, others will be attracted to you. As you instill confidence in others, they will begin to see opportunities that were previously unavailable to them. Think about it. If you have confidence and instill confidence in others that a better future is just around the corner, people will follow you and begin to grow a team that will transform their bank accounts and yours as well.

When confidence is low in tough economic times, the opportunity is great for those that can lead with a plan for a brighter future. Let's assume that 70% of the adult population is concerned about their financial future. The opportunity for you to grow as a leader is greater as you help to restore faith in others and their belief that things will get better. That is the challenge that represents our greatest opportunity. So if you are not growing personally as fast as you would like, become a great leader by reclaiming your own confidence and then helping others to see that the future is bright.

We grow by attracting others and enrolling them in a future filled with hope and the fulfillment of their dreams. So reclaim your confidence and begin to show others that today represents a real chance to help many people create a compelling future for themselves and their families. Instill confidence in others.

Your paycheck is a manifestation of the number of people that you help to see that times are tough, but it doesn't have to stay that way for long. Confidence is the key.

CHAPTER 16

How I Turn Little Square Pieces of Cardboard into $100 Bills

"Jordan, you are like a magician!" I've heard this from quite a few people. For many, what I do appears to be magic. It's really very simple. Your job as a Beach Money entrepreneur is to take the invisible and make it visible. Your job is to take something that has little to no value and make it valuable. Your job is to help others look at a situation differently and, as a result, transform their lives. Here's an example: What's the value of a business card? It's made of cardboard and ink. I pay about $50 for 1,000 cards— about a nickel a piece. I may as well treat someone's business card like the 5-cent piece of cardboard it is: throw it on my desk, stick it in a drawer, stuff it in my pocket, and forget about it.

But if you had a business card worth $50, how would you treat it? What if it were worth $100 or $1,000? Let's say you moved to the beach or to your favorite place in the mountains. During your first week there, you went around town introducing yourself to one hundred business owners and collecting one hundred business cards. According to our math, at a nickel a card you would have about $5 worth of business cards. However, if each card were worth $100 to you, you would have collected $10,000 worth of cards during your first week in town.

Here's the big question: How do you turn each of those little pieces of cardboard into $100 bills? I did a demonstration at a networking lunch recently. I collected eighteen business cards from the business owners at the meeting and laid them all out on the table at the front of the room. I then asked the questions that I have been asking you, and got similar answers.

I also asked the group, "How much business could you expect someone to do with you if they stayed with you over their entire lifetime?" Their answers varied. The lowest amount was $2,000 and the highest was $300,000. Suppose the lifetime value of a customer to me is $5,000. When I collect one hundred business cards, my job is to turn some of them into lifelong customers or distributors.

Each time I take some action, I increase the chances that one or more of my business card contacts will turn into lifelong customers or distributors.

For each one hundred cards:

If I collect one hundred business cards and just do Action 1 below, making a quick phone call to each person, and just one of them becomes a lifelong customer, then I collect $5,000 (the lifetime value of a customer); $5,000 divided by one hundred business cards means that each card is worth $50 to me. I may want to treat each card like a $50 bill!

Action	Result
1. I make a quick phone call to each	One becomes a lifelong customer
2. I make a call and send a card to each	Two become lifelong customers
3. I buy each person lunch	Three become lifelong customers
4. I send each one a gift	Four become lifelong customers
5. I send each one some business	Five become lifelong customers
6. I stay in contact with each person	Six become lifelong customers
7. I do all of the above	Ten become lifelong customers

If I collect one hundred business cards and just do Action 2, make a call and send a card to each one, and just two become lifelong customers, then I collect $10,000 (the lifetime value of a customer times 2); $10,000 divided by one hundred business cards means that each card is worth $100 to me. I may want to treat each as I would a $100 bill.

This chapter is titled, "How I Turn Little Square Pieces of Cardboard into $100 Bills." I could have called it, "How I Turned Little Square Pieces of Cardboard into $1,000 Bills." But I didn't, for two reasons. One, you wouldn't have believed me. And two, I have never seen a $1,000 bill, although I have heard they exist!

If I do a great job at each of these seven things on a regular basis for the next two years, I can expect to have ten or so new lifelong customers as a result of my attention to the true value of each person that I have met. This assumes a 10 percent success rate. However, I have seen some very skilled business owners get as high as a 40 to 50 percent success rate! When ten people become my lifetime customers, I will have collected $50,000; $50,000 divided by one hundred new business card contacts equals $500 per business card! How would you treat each card and each contact if you knew that each one was worth $500?

The lifetime value of a customer to you may be much more than $5,000. For many business owners, it is much higher. Can you see how some business owners become wealthy while others struggle their entire lifetime? This chapter alone could be worth millions of dollars to you. At the risk of being accused of "hype," I would like to share another perspective on the value of these activities. As you build relationships over time and continue to add quality lifetime customers to your network, some of these customers will result in referrals. (Remember, money does grow on trees!) So a customer with a lifetime value of $5,000 might refer two people to you who also become lifetime customers. That adds $10,000 to the $5,000 lifetime value of each customer! What was that little business card worth? You can take one hundred business cards and increase the value of each from 5 cents to $1,000 to $5,000. Now that's Beach Money!

REAL-LIFE EXAMPLE

In my current business, I have personally recruited 122 business partners. I have done about 500 presentations in three years to recruit these people. I estimate that I have collected about 3,000 business cards. The result is approximately $1.2 million per year in income ($100,000 per month). So the math shows that each recruit is worth about $840 per month. Each time I sponsor someone new, it's like increasing my income by $840 per month.

I collected about 3,000 business cards and maintained constant communication with each person through phone calls, cards, e-mails, and lunches. I built relationships and continued to look for opportunities to refer business to each person in my network. Using my simple equation, $100,000 per month divided by 3,000 business card contacts means that each card I collect is worth $33 in monthly income to me (almost $400 per year). Each time I get a business owner's card, my income goes up by $33 per month! That's pretty cool!

CHAPTER 17

The $1 Yardstick Solution

A simple wooden yardstick holds a great lesson in planning your Beach Money future. You can pick one up at the local hardware store for about a dollar.

Let's assume each inch represents two years of your life, so that yardstick represents a lifetime of seventy-two years. At about ten inches, we start our working life (20 years old). We work until we are 65 years old. That means at about thirty-two inches we begin to slow down.

The most productive years of our working lives happen between ten inches and thirty-two inches. We work and get promoted. We work and get a raise. We work and get downsized. We work and get laid off. We work to get another job. We work and get another raise. We work and get relocated. We work and get replaced. And we hope to retire with something to show for all of our work. We do this for twenty-two inches of our thirty-six-inch life.

Working life begins
Most productive years of working life
Working life ends

Financial freedom can be achieved in 4 years (2 inches)

Making money the Beach Money way allows you to do in two inches what you could not accomplish in all twenty-two inches of hard work. When you work at a job, your money stops when you stop. When you make money the Beach Money way, you can stop working and the money continues to flow into your bank account for years to come. Two inches is equal to four years. A consistent four-year commitment to making money the Beach Money way can create a monthly residual income stream that will last far into the future. After working the Beach Money way for two inches, you can enjoy the next three, five, ten, or twenty inches of your life doing what you want to do.

CHAPTER 18

How to Get Really Rich
by Breaking Even

Jay, a friend of mine, possessed wisdom that few ever attain in their lifetimes. He was older and had lots of experience running businesses and motivating people. His advice was always simple and profound.

I had a new distributor pop up in Fort Collins, Colorado. I was still working my job and was making less than $200 per month in my new business. I asked Jay whether I should go to visit this new distributor. His advice gave me a decision-making model that continues to serve me today. It applies to any business that involves training teams and leveraging the work of people and money. He said, "Ask yourself if you can make the trip break even. If the trip can break even, then anything that happens after you leave will be profit to you."

Taking Jay's advice, I decided to go. My goal was to break even. My new distributor, Donna, was married to Mike and had a little boy named Tanner. Donna used to work for a hotel in town but was now staying home to raise her little boy. She wanted a home-based business. She had big dreams. I did some simple calculations and figured that my trip would cost me about $300: $150 for airfare, $100 for a rental car, and $50 for food. Donna and Mike invited me to stay at their home, so I wouldn't need to pay for a hotel room. I made $100 each time someone signed up, so if I could help Donna recruit and train three people that weekend, my $300 trip would break even. Most of all, I would have an opportunity to spend some time with Donna, get to know her, and give her some training. That training could lead to future growth that would not require any more of my time or effort. Donna could carry the torch and continue to build a team from there.

Donna had set up about eight appointments for us to meet with some of her friends. I was very excited for Donna. She was off to a great start. Our first appointment was at 11:30 a.m. At 10 a.m., the phone rang. Donna's friend had a sick son and couldn't meet with us. We were supposed to meet our 1 o'clock appointment at the restaurant attached to the hotel where Donna used to work. We waited for thirty minutes. Donna's 1 o'clock appointment was a no-show. We tried to call, left two messages, and never got a return call.

One by one, over the next few hours, all of Donna's appointments either canceled or no-showed. Not one person followed through on their appointment time.

"Network marketing has completely changed my families life for generations to come. We went from having no hope of ever traveling the world, raising my own child, living in other areas to doing it all. Including a one-year vacation with our family, having the time to beat cancer stress free, and sit by my passing sister's bedside. Network Marketing reinvented our family mindset on how life can be lived. When you learn how to make residual-leveraged income vs transaction-based income or hourly wages, you are free to live."

DARLA DIGRANDI
Former high-end Salon & Spa Owner for
19 years with 49 employees
San Diego, California

Donna was discouraged, but I did everything I could to prop her up. She had a great attitude and didn't let this setback keep her down. But I had borrowed $300 on my credit card to take this trip, and I have to say I was a little bummed out. My goal to break even on this trip didn't quite work out.

About a month later, Donna asked me to give her another shot. But at that time $300 was a lot of money to me. Donna promised me that she would have a large group for us to meet with, but there were no guarantees. I did agree to take another trip to see Donna. I also set a goal to make up for the $300 loss from my first trip and make an additional $300 to pay for my second trip to Colorado.

Donna said she was going to rent a large room at the hotel where she used to work and invite everyone she knew to meet with us. She also wanted to spend some money and run a big ad in the local paper. Typically, ads are not the best way to launch this kind of business, but she insisted on running one. I showed up on Friday, and on Saturday morning at 9 o'clock we were all set for the "crowd." At 8:30 we made all the final preparations, including setting up the raffle prizes at the front of the room and getting the markers, name tags, and sign-in sheets in position for the throngs of guests scheduled to show up. At 9 o'clock we were still the only ones in the room. At 9:15, one used-car salesman who had seen our ad arrived (I had started to question whether the paper actually ran it!).

The used-car salesman sat in the front row and he won the raffle prize! By the way, he didn't sign up. Not one of Donna's personal guests showed up. But she had a positive attitude and had decided to succeed regardless of her setbacks. I went back to Arizona fully expecting Donna's enthusiasm to fade. I saw her going from a starry-eyed distributor with hopes for a brighter future to a weary, road-worn casualty of the network marketing war.

But over the next few months Donna was on every team conference call and worked to introduce our business to many people. Between being a mom and a wife, Donna would present the opportunity to two or three people every day. She learned the business inside and out. She became a real pro. About eight months later, Donna invited me back to meet with her group. She had over 850 people in attendance! Her checks were skyrocketing. My original $600 investment and two short trips to Colorado netted me over $30,000 in profit over the next few years.

Jay's simple advice to ask the question, "Can you make the trip break even?" has helped me in many ways. I always make my decisions based on whether an event or a trip will break even. If it can, then anything that happens after that is pure profit. I use the income from the event or trip to fund it. Sometimes my calculations are a little off and I make a little less than planned. However, usually the benefits of spending time training and building relationships with distributors far outweigh the costs involved.

I have applied this same formula to trade shows and seminars. These events are great networking opportunities. There are two approaches you can take. You can roam around meeting and collecting business cards from all the other exhibitors, or you can actually set up your own display exhibit. The first option is of course the least expensive. Setting up an exhibit can be a lot of work and it's usually pretty costly. Again, simply ask yourself, "Will the event allow me to at least break even?" If the answer is no, my recommendation is to not do it.

It's easy to get excited and begin to hallucinate about all the money you will make at a trade show event. Some can cost as much as $6,000 to $10,000 for booth rental, power, Internet, supplies, and travel. It can be a great opportunity, but not if the event won't break even for you. It is very difficult to break even at an event costing more than $1,000 total, even if you have a group splitting the expenses. So I encourage you to be smart about these trade show activities.

I am all for investing in your business. I am also for making money. You always want to budget for success. Follow Jay's advice if you want to build a profitable business. If you are running an ad, renting a trade show booth, traveling to train your distributors or build relationships just to help them grow, ask yourself, "Can I make this activity break even?" I built a multimillion-dollar business by breaking even and you can too.

CHAPTER 19

"Come Here, I Want To Show You Something!"

Many years ago, long before I had ever sponsored my first distributor, a man speaking at a seminar I attended said to his audience, "Your TV is the reason you are struggling in your business!" He went on to tell us that the average person spends 4 to 6 hours a day in front of the television set and that that time used productively could set us free financially within 3 to 5 years. I thought to myself... "What if he is right?" In fact I watched about four hours of television every day. And I was always stressed out about not having enough time to build the business! Hello!

So after the event, I went home and unplugged my TV. And over the next few months, I found myself spending much more time reading and listening to personal development. And I started giving more presentations, signing up more people and making more money! In the beginning it wasn't easy. I was tempted to plug it back in, but I refrained. After about a year, I put the TV in the closet and two years later I gave it to Good Will. I did not have a television set for about 25 years. And during those years, I made millions of dollars in network marketing. And I didn't miss my TV one bit.

Well about five years ago, I picked up a condo on the Vegas Strip with panoramic views looking north and south.

I wanted a flat screen TV to hang on the wall for watching movies when I was in town. So I went down to the big box electronics store and told the sales guy that I was looking for a

52" flat screen TV. I told him I wanted to spend about $750 for something not too fancy.

He said to me, "Come here, I want to show you something!" He waved his hand to follow him and briskly started walking down an aisle in the store. What would you do if someone said, "Come here, I want to show you something!" and started walking away from you? You would probably follow. So that's what I did.

He walked me into a private showing room where *Shrek 3-D* was playing on the big 60" screen. I sat down on the posh leather couch and put on a pair of 3-D glasses that he handed me. The sound was rich and full and the characters in the movies sprang to life and filled the room with color and motion. It was quite impressive as the donkey jumped out of the TV and practically into my lap!

I asked him, "How much?" He said, "$6500." And I said, "I'll take it!"

I have owned the 3-D TV for about five years and have watched a total of three 3-D movies on it. That comes to just over $2000 per movie! This salesperson probably does the same demo about 2-5 times a day and he probably sells 2 to 5 $6500 TV's per week! How? By just doing a simple demo.

It dawned on me that the best invitation is simple and the best presentation is a demo.

People will ask me how to invite people to take a look and I go back to my experience at the electronics store. "Come here, I want to show you something" works as well as anything I have ever seen. My invitation sounds something like this whether in person, over the phone, or in a text message. "I want to show you something that I think you may like. When can I catch you uninterrupted for about 30 minutes?"

I have been using this for over 26 years and have set up thousands of appointments using it.

And when I present, I lean towards a demo versus a presentation. If you have a product, then have your potential distributors or customers sample the product. If you have a service, consider doing a simple demo. Allow them to see the power of what you offer and how it can help them. I have found that it's much easier for your distributors to do a demo than it is to do a formal presentation.

I learned so much in 30 minutes from this salesman. He taught me to talk less and show more. He reminded me that being simple is better than being good. I also realized that he didn't do much to sell me a $6500 television. He just showed me.

CHAPTER 20

Why Most Fail

We live in a fast-paced, "I want it now" society. With online technology, access to instant information and Google, life is moving faster and faster and our attention spans are getting quite short. So many promises of "Get Rich Quick," especially around this profession, set up an expectation that if we don't make money in 2-3 months, then we can't do it or "it" doesn't work. I fell victim to this and would switch companies every year or so for over 10 years.

The #1 downfall of most network marketers is a short attention span. We are excited and we can't stand it. When the excitement wears off, we can't seem to get it back so we go on to something else. This strategy does not work in business. People that achieve their dreams don't have a short attention span. They find something they are passionate about and they focus on it through the ups and the downs for years.

If we want a meal, we pop it in the microwave or run out for fast food. If our pizza isn't delivered in 30 minutes or less, we are upset. When we want cash, we just go to the ATM and in seconds we have it in our hands. Today when we request a ride with Uber, we expect it to be there in 1-3 minutes. A 10 minute wait is unacceptable! And we expect that if we work today, we should get paid today! Compressing time frames is an important part of building a successful business. I have observed that the success of most businesses today comes as a result of collapsing inefficiencies. So speed is becoming a part of our expectation and this is the way we seem to be wired! Yet when you dig into the backgrounds of successful business owners, in most cases their success didn't happen overnight. In most cases there are a whole bunch of things that happened below the surface before we observe their meteoric rise to stardom!

Think about all the research, investment, people, time, creativity, and problem solving required prior to the launch of a rocket ship. Billions of dollars are invested prior to a successful launch. Business is no different. And you are the ultimate source of your business. Years of personal development, growth, and investment are required prior to the successful launch of most businesses. False starts, failures, and setbacks are just part of the preparation for your successful launch.

An Olympic athlete trains for YEARS prior to actual competition. Only one person goes home with the gold.

Years of research, planning, and construction go into building a high rise or a freeway prior to it being able to offer any value in the marketplace.

A prospective doctor will school for 8-10 years and invest $200,000 before earning one penny. And then they will work 15 hours per day for $100,000 per year.

With a nominal investment of $500 or so to get started in a network marketing opportunity, it's too easy to give up after 1 or 2 setbacks. I found out first hand that setbacks are no reason to throw in the towel when it comes to building a business. The strategy of throwing in the towel is not an effective business-building strategy. Successful entrepreneurs are problem solvers and have a long-term vision for their business. It's the only thing that works.

Because it is so easy to get into this business, it's easy to get out as well. A $500 investment is easy to write off when things aren't going so great. The founder of the company that has invested millions will go to the ends of the earth to be sure a company doesn't fail. They have a lot to lose. In network marketing, it's "easy come, easy go." Easy in . . . easy out! That's the benefit and the drawback of this type of business. Even in network marketing, a long-term strategy is essential.

I had a conversation with a successful diamond broker at a wedding I attended in Dana Point, California. We were talking about the difference between an "owner" and an "employee." Some company owners get frustrated because it seems their employees just don't care as much as they do. And some company founders have a goal to get the employees to think like owners. Why? Because owners will treat the business very differently than just employees. Most employees just do their jobs and then go home. When faced with a problem or challenge, it's easy for an employee to think or even say, "That's not my job!" But an owner will creatively come up with ways to not just preserve a customer but even grow the business and even solve complex problems.

Owners have a long-term perspective and understand that a lot gets invested up front for returns that may come years down the road. Building a company requires a much different mindset! America West Airlines started as a result of the deregulation of the Airline industry. The monopolies dominated the industry with power and control. America West had one leased 737 and 200 employees and most that were under 30 years old. Many were in their early 20s. Our founder decided that he wanted to take on the big guys. It was a David and Goliath story that was emotionally charged. Our employees got behind the cause and although we were all making less than $20,000 a year, we felt the ownership of the mission. As a result, we would work 12-14 hours a day. We worked to solve ownership problems and came up with creative ways to keep expenses down and grow the airline as a cohesive team. It was fun, challenging, and extremely rewarding. We grew to over 15,000 employees and 100 jets in six short years! Apple computers did the same thing when it took on Microsoft. They were the underdog and built a company for the individual. To this day, their employees feel like owners.

Imagine planting twenty oak trees by digging holes and placing an acorn in each hole. There won't be much shade in the first year or two! If you become impatient expecting shade too soon, you may kill the baby plants! Imagine getting paid $1000 a month once the trees are five feet tall. And then getting paid $5000 a month once the trees reach 50 feet. At 100 feet you are making $10,000 a month. At 250 feet when the trees have their own acorns that fall to sprout new trees from the parent trees, you are making $20,000 a month. And when those new trees grow to eventually reach 250 feet, at maturity the trees begin to drop acorns, you are now making $100,000 a month. Do you have the patience for your plants to grow into mature trees and then eventually spawn new plants. An oak tree will take years to mature but will produce shade and acorns for many more years after that.

The #1 downfall of network marketers is a short attention span. The average business builder does one of two things. They either build for a short time and have a setback and quit or they build for a short time, have a setback and take a two-week to two-month break and then get re-energized only to do it all over again. 80%

plus of your distributors don't stand a chance because of a short attention span. We can change that by first making everyone aware that this is a problem.

Here are 3 things to prevent or fix the problem of a short attention span.

1. REALIZE THAT YOU ARE A COMPANY OWNER - This is your business and as a business owner you must have a long-term perspective and run your business as a long-term enterprise vs something you are just trying. A company owner that is building something substantial would not be dabbling in the business. When faced with challenges, they don't think about quitting. They instead think about all the ways to solve the problem and get past it. Sometimes that requires a radical change in thinking or environment. There are solutions to every problem. Your job is to find solutions and learn the lessons necessary to get past the problems.

2. STAY CLOSE TO THE FIRE - Stay connected to those people that are on a mission to change the world with your program. There are people in the company that would never consider quitting. Be around those people on a regular basis. This is one big reason to attend the regional and national events. Not participating in company events can mean business suicide.

3. LET IT GO - To survive the long haul you must learn to let go of the things you can not control and refresh your excitement each day. Hitting the "refresh" button on your business is essential to long-term success. This is a learned and conscious skill. Reinvent yourself daily.

CHAPTER 21

Managing Your Team

How do you manage such a large group of people? I know that some people actually won't build a business because they are convinced that it will just take too much time to manage a team. Not a day goes by that someone doesn't say, "You work sooooo hard!" First, I want to share with you how hard I work, and second, I want to share with you why you don't need to work hard to build a large Beach Money income.

When I work, I am extremely focused. Unless you are my close friend, you won't hear from me when I'm not working because, I'M NOT WORKING! When I'm working, you might hear from me all the time. I schedule my time off and when I'm off, I'm off! Here is my typical schedule:

1. I work about four hours per day. During my work I will be doing three-way calls with members of my team, sharing my opportunity, holding a small group meeting or training, doing a Web seminar ("webinar"), answering e-mails, or returning calls. The other twenty hours per day, I sleep, work out, socialize, study, read, travel, and so on.

2. Once a week I take two to three days off and go to the mountains. I may take an hour or two to return calls and answer e-mails.

3. About once every two months, I take one week off for some sort of trip, vacation, or training (not one or two weeks per year like a normal job).

Here are some of the trips I took in the last twelve months:

1. Europe – 1 week
2. Caribbean cruise – 1 week
3. Tony Robbins's Unleash the Power Workshop – 1 week
4. Tony Robbins's Date with Destiny Workshop – 1 week
5. Chicago to visit my family – 2 weeks
6. Venice Beach, California – 30 days spread out over 12 months

This does not include the two to three days off per week in the mountains of Arizona. Yes, if this is work, I work soooo hard!

So how is it possible to work so little and manage all of these people? If you are currently building or planning on building a big team, this is probably the most important part of this book. Your job when sponsoring someone is to simply get them started. It is not your job to manage them. Each person who joins you is an independent business owner and is responsible for his or her own business. If you plan on managing thousands of people, you will have a big problem. There are not enough hours in the day. The formula for burnout is a belief that you must manage your whole team.

If you are moving quickly in your new business, you may personally bring in about one new person per week. I don't recommend sponsoring more than one per week if you plan on doing a good job getting your new distributors started.

1. You sign them up.
2. You train them for one hour.
3. You help them bring in their first two or three people.

That's it! Any other phone calls or visits are strictly social or a periodic coaching call.

It is not your job to manage your people. If you need to manage all of your people and their people, your group will only grow as far as you can reach (arm's length). You will limit your growth to only the people you can personally work with. Think about it: how big will your group really become if all of your organizational growth depends on you? Again, your job is simply to get your new distributor started, and then go work with someone new!

It is not your job to answer the questions of all the people in your group. Your job is to train your new people to answer the questions of their new people. Everyone is responsible for the few people they bring in. If I had to manage the thousands of people in my entire group, I would go crazy!

You will never abandon your people, but you do need to delegate the responsibility for new distributors to the person who

"Network marketing creates an even playing field for anyone with the desire for success regardless of their financial, educational, or cultural background. As a result of this profession, I have been able to develop a passive income that has allowed me to relocate to the beautiful Pacific Northwest. I'm blessed to have the freedom of a business that travels with me wherever I go!"

MARK HERDERING
Former Yellow Pages salesman,
four-figure monthly earner in network marketing
Portland, Oregon

signed them up. Occasionally there will be times when a distributor is not very active in the business and may need to lean on you to pick up the loose ends of training a new person. Be careful about crippling your group by always doing it for them.

If you find yourself "spinning plates," you will have a tough time growing a large business, because you limit the number of people you can work with. Most likely you will experience burnout within a short time. Your job is to sign them up, train them, and help them sign up their first few people so they know how to do it. That's it. Then do it again and again.

REPLACE YOURSELF

Here's a way to turbocharge your team. Your goal is to replace yourself quickly. At my last job, I had a great boss. His name was Jack Birnbaum. Although I was never well suited to jobs, I learned a lot of lessons that I carried into my network marketing career. Jack gave me some advice on leadership. He said that if I wanted to become a successful manager in corporate America, I needed to find ways to quickly replace myself. Jack told me I needed to work myself out of a job! Replacing myself meant finding and training others to do my job better than I could do it. I wasn't sure if I agreed with him, but I did trust his judgment. I was a little concerned that teaching others to do what I do might ultimately mean losing my job altogether. In a way this was true. I did lose my job.

In reality, I learned that by training others to do my job, I became more valuable to my company. Yes, I would lose my job, only to be offered a better opportunity. As I helped others become more valuable in the workplace, I became more valuable to the company.

Most managers never learn this simple truth. Jack's lesson helped me to become a great trainer and leader. My company promoted me twice and gave me more responsibility.

I learned this lesson when I was in my early twenties, not knowing the impact it would have on my future. I took this message right into my network marketing career. Today, my goal is to quickly replace myself by teaching people to do what I do. By replacing myself, I become more valuable as a leader. As I become more valuable, I make more money. How does replacing yourself make you more valuable in network marketing? By replacing yourself, you are helping others get what they want.

As you train others to do what you do, they are now positioned to earn more money and to establish a Beach Money lifestyle for themselves. You are rewarded for helping others get what they want.

CHAPTER 22

Network Marketing Do's and Don'ts

When I was a child I had a children's book my mother would read to me called "This Is What Would Happen If Everybody Did!" It was an illustrated book that showed some type of bad behavior exhibited by a child on the left hand page followed by the consequence of that bad behavior on the right hand page. For example, the left page would say, "Stomp on the Cat," showing a child stomping on a cat and the right page, "This is what would happen if everybody did!" showing a bunch of freaked-out, stomped-on cats all over the page. Then the left page would say, "Leave a mess," showing a child not picking up his things and then on the right page "This is what would happen if everybody did!" showing a world with clutter and trash everywhere! I think it taught me the meaning of consequences.

Let's look at what not to do in your network marketing business. There is a hilarious skit that famous comedian Bob Newhart did where he plays a psychiatrist and a patient comes in with some complaints and in need of some counseling. Bob Newhart's advice to him was stop it!!! and then he charges his patient a ridiculous amount of money for the advice! It's actually worth watching because it offers some obvious but helpful advice for building your business. You can Google, Bob Newhart "Stop It!"

If I were to catch you doing some of these things I may yell at you to stop it!! Just stop it!!

DON'T DO THESE THINGS:

1. DON'T MAKE EXCUSES FOR WHAT YOU DO - In other words, never ever apologize for being part of the network marketing profession. You are better off facing it head on with confidence and conviction than beating around the bush. It's time to stop avoiding the topic. It's a real business with real potential and it has benefits that are astoundingly appealing to many business owners once they understand it. Don't tip toe or tap-dance around this business model. And if someone starts to give you a hard time, have some self respect and with some posture you turn them down first. No more cowering or being wimpy. You don't need to fight with them, but stand up for what you believe in and don't back down. Network marketing is one of the best kept secrets in business today. It's time that we come out of the closet. Stop apologizing!! Stop it!!!

2. DON'T CUT CORNERS ON THE IMPORTANT THINGS - This is a big one. Some days I want to shout, "Ahhhhhhhh!" (with lots of H's!!). When I learn of someone that buys a convention ticket and then tries to sell it in their company or team Facebook group. It breaks my heart because I know that if that person would just bite the bullet and go, it could transform his or her life forever. And many times not going is a death sentence in the business. Not going to your company convention is a bad idea. And buying a ticket to go and then not going is also a bad idea if you want success in your business. Cut corners when it comes to Starbucks. Cut corners when it comes to eating out. Cut corners when it comes to the cable bill (downgrade to a lower package or eliminate it altogether!). Cut corners when it comes to completing the remodeling project. Even cut corners on Christmas gifts . . .

but don't negotiate with your future. Don't cut corners on your personal development. Don't cut corners on attending your annual convention. Don't cut corners on tools. I can honestly say that one of the reasons I am here today is because I never took shortcuts when it came to investing in myself and in my business.

3. DON'T QUIT WHEN THINGS GET TOUGH - One thing I can guarantee. Things will get tough. And you will want to quit. You will want to quit many times. And I have seen people quit at all different levels. I know lots of people who quit before making any money at all. And I even have a friend that quit that was making over $100,000 a month. He got into a fight with the founder of his company and he chose to walk away from a $1.5 million-a-year business. People quit at all levels. People quit for their own reasons. I also know that the number one reason for failure in the business is throwing in the towel. Most every failed network marketing business happened because someone chose to call it quits. And almost one-hundred percent of the time it was when things got too difficult to continue. This is when your most valuable lessons are learned. No one is immune. You will think that your situation is different but it is not. Never look back. You may need to hit the reset button on your business every week but never ever quit. Quitting is not a good strategy for success.

4. DON'T GO ALL THE WAY ON THE FIRST DATE - A relationship must come before marriage. Focus on getting to know the other person and understanding a little about what makes them tick. I know you are excited and you want to share your business with the world. You'll have a better chance of acceptance if you get to know the other person before you tell them all about the business. Just sayin. If you find yourself "presenting" all over

the other person and you don't know anything about them, stop it!!

5. DON'T SAY, "I JUST GOT INTO THIS NEW LITTLE BUSINESS . . ." - It's not a new little business. This statement plants a seed in the mind of your potential distributor that what we have here is not such a big deal. It is a big deal. It's a multimillion enterprise that is transforming a generation of business people. Do you realize that your little business could someday have 1,000,000 customers in it? Do that calculation. Conservatively, your checks would be hundreds of thousands of dollars a month. That scenario is conceivable. "I just got into this new little business" really does your business no justice! Stop using this phrase.

6. DON'T TALK ABOUT THE BUSINESS - Talking about the business can be the kiss of death. First of all, it doesn't usually work because the person you are talking to hasn't seen what you have seen. People need to see it. I don't know about you, but I have caught myself a number of times beginning to tell people about the business and I can see them drifting away as I continue to explain more and more. I try and catch myself when this happens. Instead, I tell them I will get with them soon and then I just drop it. As we are parting, I say, "I may get in touch with you and we'll set up a time to chat" Then I text them and set up a time to show them everything from start to finish. Giving people the business in bits and pieces is not effective or professional. Refrain from talking about it. Set up a time to meet and take a full 30 minutes to one hour to show all of it to them from start to finish.

7. DON'T DO NOTHING - Imagine a business where everyone did nothing (This is What Would Happen If Everybody Did!). You would be part of a company with no growth. Your

business starts with you. Always. Doing something is always better than doing nothing. So you are better off doing it horribly wrong than not doing it at all. Why? Because at least when you are doing it wrong you will get feedback that will teach you what not to do. So rather than waiting around doing nothing, do something. What I have observed is that most people do nothing. And guess what the result is of the people that do nothing? You guessed right . . . nothing. So a big don't in this business is don't do nothing! On a day you find yourself doing nothing, catch yourself and go do something. Try and do something that will advance your business. Look through your friend list on FB and send 10 messages asking each person to take a look at what you are doing. You could even say, "If I were to send you a video about a way to make money, would you watch it?" Now this wouldn't be my first choice to show the business, but it's way better than doing nothing!!

8. DON'T STALK OR BUG PEOPLE THAT TELL YOU NO - I was at an event recently that had about two hundred business owners. A young professional photographer walked up to me and we talked for a few minutes. She asked me what I did. I told her and I may have well said I was a vampire . . . the cross came out!! She gave me three reasons in about 10 seconds why she would never do my business. I was like . . . "Whoa! Whoa! Whoa! I have no interest in recruiting you! You just asked me what I did and I told you!" She calmed down and we talked. I asked her a bunch of questions about her business and everyone left happy. But I realized the reason this happened is because she told one person in the group that she was uninterested yet that person kept trying to recruit her! Don't do that! Stop trying to recruit people that tell you no. They know you want them. Stay in touch. Be kind.

Be generous. And look for ways that you can help them grow. They will watch you and it's possible over time that they will come to you when they are ready if you keep the doors open. If you find yourself chasing, stalking, groveling, bothering, or begging others to join you in your business, stop it!!

9. DON'T SETTLE - Most people shrink their dreams down to meet income instead building their income up to meet their dreams. Settling means giving up on your life. You were born to fly. I was told once that God will not give us dreams that we weren't meant to fulfill. Sometimes it takes the wind out of me when I watch people stop fighting for what they want and buying in to the small thinking that is all around them. Settling is defeat. Settling is giving up. Winners don't give up. And most people settle. Most people stop trying. Most people lose heart. And this is why most people don't make it. But this doesn't have to be you. Stop selling out. Stop settling. Stop buying in to the negativity. Which sounds better . . . "(insert your name) Steve didn't settle. He wasn't a sell out. It was tough but he persevered. And today Steve has his dream life" OR "Steve settled. He decided he didn't want to work that hard. He didn't see the job through and his dreams slipped away forever. He's older now and has lots of regrets. He'll never have a second chance. Oh well." Which story is most inspiring?

These are your network marketing don'ts. If you catch yourself doing any of these things, stop it!! Just stop!!

CHAPTER 23

Strategies for Creating Beach Money

BEACH MONEY STRATEGY #1:
FOCUS ON DISTRIBUTION VERSUS SALES.

One big myth about network marketing is that you need to be very good at sales to succeed. This is completely false.

I know many people with terrible sales skills who have created fantastic wealth in network marketing. In fact, sales skills have very little to do with creating a Beach Money lifestyle. Over the years I have seen lots of successful, well-seasoned salespeople join network marketing companies and fall flat on their faces over and over again. I can't even count the number of phone conversations I've had with skillful, well-meaning sales professionals who tout their extensive sales experience and amazing production numbers. Not a week goes by that I don't hear statements like, "I have been the number one sales producer at my company for the past three years" or "I've sold over $2 million in product since starting with my company!" My experience has shown that those strong track records in sales mean very little in network marketing. The fact is a sales background may even slow you down.

Don't get me wrong, I love the sales profession. But I know that a focus on sales will yield you very little in our industry. Selling can certainly give you a nice income, but it is linear in nature. To make money in sales, you have to continue to sell month after month. If you stop selling you stop making money! When I talk about Beach Money, I'm talking about "walk-away" income.

Beach Money gives you the freedom to stop working and still get paid. Selling to new customers month after month contradicts the ultimate objective, which is to eventually retire on the beach or wherever you choose to hang out!

The first strategy for creating the freedom that comes with Beach Money is to focus on distribution rather than on sales. Distribution is the system of creating multiple points of sale. Rather than aiming to get as many sales as possible, your goal is to have lots and lots of people making a few sales each.

Here are two offers that illustrate the difference between sales and distribution:

- **Offer 1:** I will offer you one-liter bottles of soda for $1 each. You can buy as many as you want from me. These one-liter bottles will retail for $2 each. Again, you may buy as many as you like at the $1 wholesale price. Would you want this offer? Most salespeople would love to have this opportunity! The focus here is on sales, and a good salesperson could make lots of money with this offer, but he will probably never retire on the beach unless he shifts his focus to distribution.

- **Offer 2:** I will sell you one vending machine for $1,000 that will dispense sodas at $1 each. You will earn 10 cents for each soda sold out of the machine. Do you want this machine? You may want it or not. I will also purchase all of the product you need to stock your machine. I will even stock your machine for you! Now, do you want this machine? More likely! When you buy this vending machine from me for $1,000 I will also include lifetime maintenance on the machine. You will never have to fix it if it breaks. The offer is sounding even better! As part of my offer to you, I will collect all of the money from the machine, count it, and tabulate an accounting report for you. You then get the report and a check from me each month. That's not all. I will give you an unlimited opportunity to collect a commission on sales from multiple vending machines in unlimited locations around the country and eventually around the world. You only need to purchase one machine. I will buy all of the product, stock the machines, maintain the machines, collect the money, count the money, put together a report, and send you a check. The only thing you will need to do is get me as many locations as you can. You will receive 10 cents for each soda sold by each of the vending machines in your network. Do you want this offer? Who wouldn't take it?

Of course, to make lots of money you need to arrange to have hundreds of machines placed in many locations. But you're only required to buy one machine yourself. You don't need to buy the product. You don't need to stock the machines. You don't need to maintain the machines. You don't need to collect the money from the machines. You don't need to count the money or even create an accounting report. In fact, you don't even need to place any of the other machines. Imagine getting paid 10 cents for each soda sold out of every one of your machines. What if you have 1,000 to 4,000 machines placed all around the country?

For this offer to work for you, you must focus on the distribution of the machines. You find others to buy machines and teach them to do the same thing that you are doing. That's it. Your job is not to sell sodas; it's to market the distribution of the machines.

This is a very important distinction. It determines whether this is just another sales job or whether you create a distribution network that gives you a Beach Money lifestyle.

As your network of machines and machine distributors grows, you get a percent of the 10 cent commission paid on each soda sold. You split that 10 cents with other distributors of the machines. Your "take" is essentially free money, because your involvement is limited. Your job is just to get people started placing machines and training them on the system.

In network marketing, you buy a distribution center at a one-time cost of somewhere between $100 and $1,000. You might choose to buy some product each month for your own personal use and maybe to sell to a few close friends, but that's it. Your cash investment is very low compared to most traditional businesses. After that, you won't need to purchase any more distribution centers. Your host company will do everything for you except for marketing new distribution centers. That's your job. Create lots of points of distribution that each sell product, and you'll make lots of money.

In Offer 1 above, you get to buy the product at a great wholesale price of $1 and resell it at $2. But to make money, you have to keep selling the product. There is no time for the beach. In Offer 2, you help to create lots of points of distribution. Imagine that each soda machine is a distributor in your network. The host company will produce and distribute the product and collect all the money. The host company will generate accounting reports with a breakdown of sales and commissions. The host company will even manage the genealogy of your network. You will simply help the company create multiple points of distribution and they will send you a few pennies on each unit of product sold through your distribution network. This is genuine Beach Money! As your network grows, your income grows. You get the best of all worlds.

If you are good at sales, that's fine, but the first strategy for creating the freedom that comes with Beach Money is to focus your efforts on distribution. Build a distribution network of people who each buy a little product and sell to a few repeat customers.

BEACH MONEY STRATEGY #2:
FOCUS ON PASSIVE, NONLINEAR INCOME VERSUS ACTIVE, LINEAR INCOME.

You always get what you focus on. I can't emphasize this enough. If you are working toward getting a better job or getting a raise from your boss, you will never have a Beach Money lifestyle. Getting raises and moving up in an organization are fine if you want to work for the rest of your life. But if you are looking to have more free time to live your life the way you envision it, you must immediately shift your focus to an opportunity that pays you passive, nonlinear income. Don't wait. Do it now. There is a learning curve here and by getting involved in a part-time opportunity right away, you will begin acquiring the mind-set and skills necessary to produce your Beach Money lifestyle.

Don't just talk about it. Don't just plan for it. Don't just read about it. Take immediate action. Once you get in the game and surround yourself with like-minded people, you will begin to move toward the life of your dreams. Ask yourself, "If I work at this for the next five years and then stop working, will I be able to live comfortably in the locale of my choice (the beach, the mountains, the desert)?" If the answer is no, then find an opportunity immediately that can create the passive, nonlinear income you need.

BEACH MONEY STRATEGY #3:
BECOME THE MOST WELL-CONNECTED PERSON YOU KNOW.

To be a Beach Money entrepreneur, you must attract well-connected people. A well-connected person is someone who has lots of great relationships with the people in his or her network. Well-connected people don't need much help in growing a network quickly, because their network is already in place. They have already established strong ties of trust and can easily and quickly assemble a team. Successful people are well connected and attract other successful people. So the best way to attract well-connected people is to be one.

When I was in my early twenties, I made a personal choice to be the one with the big Rolodex. I wanted to be known as the person who had the connections in case anyone needed something from me. I built a huge Rolodex and created relationships with

"Of all the entrepreneurial opportunities available today, the best is network marketing. It gives common people the chance, with very little risk, to build an income-generating business that can produce financial and time freedom. I grew up dirt poor with no dad, taught math, and coached basketball for 16 years, and always struggled financially. However, because of network marketing, I have been blessed to make millions of dollars, live an amazing lifestyle, and help thousands of people improve their lives. You can be, do, and have more with network marketing!"

PRESLEY SWAGERTY
Multimillion Dollar Yearly Earner
Dallas, Texas

many successful entrepreneurs. If someone needed a publisher, I knew a publisher. If someone needed an interior designer, I knew a great interior designer. If someone needed a good roofer, I could quickly introduce them to an exceptional roofer.

As a result of being a well-connected Beach Money entrepreneur, I can now quickly and easily call on anyone in my network and ask them for a favor. I rarely ask for favors, but when I call on someone in my network and ask them to take a look at an opportunity, most will immediately say yes because I have built a reputation of integrity and trustworthiness. Not everyone will partner with me. But the ones who do are well-connected people who can have a big impact right from the start.

BEACH MONEY STRATEGY #4:
BE SURE YOUR ENVIRONMENT SUPPORTS YOUR CAUSE.

I think I might have been born an entrepreneur. My mom tells me she remembers me continually inventing things around the house. I'd take random household items like toilet paper rolls, Elmer's Glue, and marbles and build contraptions to show my friends. Once I set up a lemonade stand and offered customers a free refill for an extra nickel. Even way back then I was looking for ways to collect more money from my customers by increasing the value of my offering. By the time I had a paper route I was looking for ways to increase my tips by giving personal attention. In fact, tips became the most exciting part of my paper route business.

I had the qualities of an entrepreneur even as a small boy, but my father had a regular job and so did the parents of all of my friends. I do not remember having any models of entrepreneurship in my life. Our family never talked about owning a business.

After college I began to see that I was an entrepreneur stuck in a job person's body. I was always drawn to the idea of creating things, building things, and making money. But my environment never supported those interests. Growing up I was constantly ridiculed for my crazy ideas. I always felt pulled in two different directions. My spirit would pull me toward starting a business, but most of my friends and family would tell me I was a nutcase. This tug of war went on for years. At times I felt like an alien. I know that you can probably relate to this, because you are reading this book! As I started meeting other people like me, I realized I was not alone. Many shared my entrepreneurial drive, but because they didn't run in my circles I had never gotten to know them. Most of them had been ridiculed and made fun of as children as well. I began to realize that I really wasn't crazy. I had been given a gift. I was being led to the exciting, ever-changing world of free enterprise. But my environment had never supported my cause, so now I needed to surround myself with like-minded people who could relate to what I was up to in my life.

I was talking with a young woman recently about being in business. She was in her early twenties and had already tried a number of different endeavors. When she told people about her ideas, they were usually pessimistic and told her all the reasons why her ideas wouldn't fly. Then she'd get stressed out and question whether she should pursue her dreams. She had been trained as a school teacher, and her latest idea was to start a business tutoring gifted children. Since most of the people around her were not business owners and didn't have business minds, they didn't really understand what she was up to or why she wanted to be in business for herself. So once again she got excited about her idea only to be attacked by people who didn't get it. This pattern had become a constant source of anxiety for her.

Start surrounding yourself with other like-minded people right away. Make friends with other entrepreneurs. You'll find that when you are around other people who are also building businesses, you will get the encouragement and support you are looking for. You will also learn how to handle the emotional ups and downs that come with being in business for yourself. Read the biographies and autobiographies of successful business builders. You will see that most of them had ideas that were unconventional—even outrageous—and that the majority were also subjected to ridicule from friends and family.

Phases of acceptance:

1. When you first share your business idea, you are labeled as crazy.
2. Once you have some success, you are labeled as visionary.
3. When your business idea makes you wealthy, you are labeled as lucky.

Realizing that I am different from most people was a breakthrough for me. I think differently, and although there are many people who think like I do (you are probably one of them!) there are many more who don't. I choose to surround myself with the people who support what I am up to in business. You'll soon be able to quickly spot the people who have the qualities of an entrepreneur. They are the ones you want to be around.

About once every two or three months, I take retreats with other successful business owners. We usually go to fun places (many have beaches!) like Lake Tahoe, San Diego, and Hawaii. We share stories and discuss investment and partnership ideas. We gain inspiration from each other. Most of all, we find comfort in knowing that we are all part of a special group of people who have the gift of an entrepreneurial spirit.

BEACH MONEY STRATEGY #5:
MAKE FRIENDS WITHOUT AN AGENDA.

I have a lot of friends. Most of them do business with me. But if I had pursued their friendships to get them to do business with me, I would not have many friends.

Make friends to make friends, not to get business. If you make friends to get business, you will lose friends as fast as you made them. And you will probably not get much business.

My friends love to do business with me because I respect our friendship and don't exploit our relationship for personal gain. I sometimes get asked, "How do you approach friends about your business opportunity?" I never really approach my existing friends about business. I do need to make sure they know what I am doing in case they are interested or want to refer people to me. Just like I may share a hobby or an exciting story, I want to tell them what I am up to. But I do not go after them or try to recruit them.

What's the difference between telling someone what you do and trying to get them into your business? Really, it's all about your intention. I am not sharing my business with them to get them involved. I want to hear about their triumphs and challenges. I want to hear about the kids and their last vacation. I also want to know if they have started any new businesses. Telling your friends about what you do does not exploit your friendships.

Imagine finding out that a friend of yours was involved in a business that was making him $8,000 per month. How would you feel if you found out that he had an opportunity that he could share with you but never did?

When I tell someone what I'm up to and they start asking questions, they've expressed interest and given me permission to continue. At this point, I may give them more information, answer their questions, and even invite them to take a look at my business if they want to.

BEACH MONEY STRATEGY #6:
CREATE MEMORABLE EXPERIENCES FOR YOURSELF AND FOR OTHERS.

Relationships are the glue that holds a team together. Teams that play together stay together. There is nothing like getting together with a bunch of people who share a common vision. By anchoring these gatherings with fun experiences, you can create strong positive associations that will last a lifetime. Your team will remember these experiences and share them with others. When people are having fun, they want to stick around. Everyone wants to be part of a team that's having fun!

One of the most valuable things you can do for yourself and your team is to bring groups together in fun and positively stimulating environments. I've even found that there is no need to structure training around these gatherings. The experience of sharing stories, laughing, telling jokes, and swapping inspiring tips will do more for your team than any training you can provide.

Have parties for your team, schedule trips together, meet for coffee on a Saturday morning, go skiing, have an overnight retreat, or take a cruise together. You don't need to pay for the people on your team to attend these get-togethers. Just organize the trip and have them pay their own way. Consider doing a special dinner for your group prior to a corporate training event or convention. And think about having a couple of these gatherings at the beach!

I recommend doing at least one of these gatherings each month. You can grow a huge organization by getting people together on a regular basis just to have fun. Have the members of your team invite guests. Most of the guests will end up becoming part of your team. Everyone loves to have fun! You can be the catalyst for creating fun and memorable experiences for your team. As your team grows into other cities, encourage your leaders to do exactly the same thing!

If your team is very small, that's okay. Start small. Get together with three or four people to rent a motivational movie and order pizza. This is how we work! Just as a side note, these gatherings are essential to building your business. That means you get to write them off as legitimate business expenses on your tax return!

BEACH MONEY STRATEGY #7:
INVEST IN YOURSELF AND IN OTHERS.

I once was told by a top income earner that for each person I have at a company convention, I could multiply my group by 100 one year later. This seemed outrageous, but I believed he might be telling me the truth. So I found two very motivated distributors who seemed to be having some financial struggles getting started. I paired them together and offered to buy their convention tickets. I also told them that they could split the hotel room. These two guys attended the convention and went on to build a group of thousands! Now each year I grant some convention tickets to a few of the right people. There are no guarantees, but when you invest in yourself and in your people, you can never go wrong.

One year I read a book called *The Choice* by Og Mandino. I loved the book so much that I bought one hundred copies to share with all of my leaders as a holiday gift. I have found that a thoughtful gesture and an example of giving can go a long way toward strengthening a team.

I have budgeted 5 percent of my income for personal development. I purchase books and CDs each month that feed my need for personal growth. I have noticed that when I work on myself, I tend to attract others who are also working on themselves. These are exactly the type of people I want on my team! I also attend at least two or three week-long training events each year. I meet many other inspiring leaders and grow to new levels of achievement each time I attend.

I have heard struggling distributors say that they can't afford to buy anything yet. This is a poor excuse and it will hold you back in your personal growth and development. You are an entrepreneur. Entrepreneurs are creative and resourceful. Go to the library or split the cost with another distributor until you can afford to buy the books or CDs yourself. There are many opportunities to attend free seminars offered by network marketing companies. Don't miss out on the chance to grow immeasurably by being around other top leaders in your business. Successful Beach Money entrepreneurs are generous with their time and money. They consistently invest in themselves and in others.

BEACH MONEY STRATEGY #8: DREAM.

I have had the good fortune to get to know two billionaires. I have also spent hundreds of hours with multimillionaires in their homes. While they have very different personalities, I have noticed a few things they all have in common:

1. They have big dreams and they talk about their dreams.
2. They have magazines and photo albums on their coffee tables and desks that contain some of the things that they dream about.
3. They read books and listen to CDs that help to expand their dreams.

Coming from a lower-middle-income neighborhood where big dreams were not a topic of discussion, I guess I never really expected to see this. I remember sitting on the couch at the 14,000 square foot home of one of the billionaires. On his coffee table were a horse ranch magazine and a private jet magazine. As I sat thumbing through the magazines, he told me about his dreams to acquire horse ranches and private jets.

You may not be dreaming about big homes, jets, or horse ranches. Maybe you're inspired by different dreams. What matters is that you get really comfortable with the images of what you want. You must begin to feel what it would be like to experience your dreams once they are in your life.

I have met many people who have stopped dreaming. I can ask any one of them to write down ten things they would like to have in their life, and they will have a hard time coming up with them. As children they almost certainly had big dreams. As they grew up, they probably had family and friends tell them over and over again that they were not being realistic. Ultimately they have given up on their dreams.

I am giving you permission to dream again. Decide today to let go of your doubts about what is possible and begin to rebuild your dream muscles. What would your perfect life look like? How would it feel? Who would be in it? What would you be doing? I know no one who has built a successful business without a clear idea of what it would be like to live the life of his or her dreams.

BEACH MONEY STRATEGY #9:
ACT AND ADJUST; DON'T ANALYZE.

Analyzing is a process of logic. Understand that your success will not be logical. Most great success stories defy logic. There will be no past evidence for your growth. As you grow, your journey takes you into uncharted territory. You have probably never been there before. As good as you may be at analyzing all the variables, you will not be able to figure everything out in advance. You will be thrown many curve balls. How you handle them will determine how well you do on the journey. Your paycheck will be your measuring stick.

Think about it. Going from working at a job to living the Beach Money life will be a brand new experience for you. There is currently no evidence in your life that this can happen. But do you realize that nearly everyone who has created a financially free life did it with no evidence that it was possible for them either?

You know what you want. Most likely, even if you think you have it all figured out, it won't happen the way you think it will. When the company I had been with for thirteen years went away, I thought it was the end of the world. Little did I know that my first million-dollar year would come from a company I had no interest in at the beginning. If my last company had not gone away, I wouldn't be writing this book! The journey to success almost never unfolds the way you expect it to. Trying to analyze it and figure it out just delays your success. Act now and adjust along the way! Trust that you will learn the lessons you need to learn. You will not be able to plan it all out in advance. But the sooner you start taking action toward your dreams, the sooner you will start living your Beach Money life.

BEACH MONEY STRATEGY #10:
FOCUS ON YOUR PEOPLE SKILLS MORE THAN YOUR TECHNOLOGY SKILLS.

Typically the people who create the technology work for the ones who have the people skills. Get really good with people by being around others who are great with people. Leadership is the most valuable skill you can have for creating a Beach Money life. Technology is vitally important and I am grateful that not everyone wants to lead people, or there would be no one left to handle the technical stuff. I couldn't run my business without the people who thrive on working at technology. I pay them well and treat them with the highest regard.

However, if you are looking for a large Beach Money income and you have a choice between building your team or building a Web site, I'd advise you to spend your time learning to build a team and influence people in a positive way. You can always hire the computer experts to run your technology. Most wealthy people I know don't even answer their own e-mails!

Read books such as *How to Win Friends and Influence People* by Dale Carnegie and *The Magic of Thinking Big* by David Schwartz. Become a master of communications, networking, building relationships, and public speaking. As you develop your leadership and communication skills, you'll find you will be in high demand as an expert team builder and you'll get paid big money for doing it!

BEACH MONEY STRATEGY #11:
OUTSOURCE AS MUCH AS POSSIBLE.

One of my specific goals as my team grew into the thousands was to stay outsourced. In other words, I wanted to free up as much of my time as possible. Rather than trying to learn to do everything, I paid others to do what I couldn't do or wasn't willing to learn. It took me years to figure out that my time is best spent building my business and not doing manual labor or tedious, un-interesting tasks. I have never been good at keeping track of my accounting records. I don't enjoy cleaning things. I have no inter-est in learning how to fix a car. Things I don't enjoy drain my en-ergy and take me longer to do than someone who loves the work.

My bookkeeper, Carrie Putman of Bookkeeping Helpers, saved my life. Yet the day I set her up to do my record keeping and bill paying, I thought I would lose it. The idea of giving up control of my financial record keeping made me so nervous. Within forty-five days I realized it was the best business decision I had ever made. It completely freed me up from something that caused me so much stress each month. Not only that, I just wasn't very good at it and was always inaccurate. Carrie and I have grown together and today she handles my entire estate record keeping and pays all of my bills.

In the beginning, you might start by hiring a house cleaner to come in twice a month. As your business grows, you can increase the frequency. Very simply, pay others to do what you don't want to do or what you are not very good at.

Don't lie to yourself about what you like to do. In other words, if you really dislike landscaping but don't have the money to hire a landscaper, don't try to convince yourself that you do your own landscaping for the exercise. You can always go to the gym for exercise! Instead, work on building up your business to the point where you can hire out the landscaping to someone who loves it! For every task that you don't like to do, there is someone out there who will do it for you for a small fee, and probably enjoy doing it. This is not about being lazy or pretentious. It's about freeing up your time so you can do what you love and spend time at the beach with your family!

BEACH MONEY STRATEGY #12:
KEEP YOUR MESSAGE SIMPLE AND CONSISTENT.

I met a guy who taught me the value of simplicity. He built an organization of over two million distributors in a ten-year period. I figured he knew something about duplication. I used to bring people to hear him speak all over the country as I was getting my business going. He would speak for one hour in each city. He said exactly the same thing each time he spoke. He never changed his message. I probably heard him speak over a hundred times. Each time, I heard the exact same message. It almost seemed too simple. After hearing him for the third time, I actually became kind of bored with his message.

But my new distributors were hearing his message for the first time and they were not bored at all. They were both relieved and excited to hear how simple our business was! I figured if it was good enough for him, it was good enough for me. So I started sharing the same message with my distributors. My team started to grow!

He used to say, when you add extra stuff to the message, it slows down your growth. He taught a basic three-step plan (sound familiar?):

1. Get a few distributors.
2. Get a few customers.
3. Help your distributors get started doing the same thing.

Whenever someone asked him a question with a complicated answer, he would say, "I'm not really sure, but if you will go out and get a few distributors, teach them to get a few customers, and help your distributors get started doing the same thing, the company will send you some money!"

Now, I know that he knew the answers to those questions, but he wouldn't answer them. He would just refocus each person's attention back to the three basic things that would cause their group to grow so they could make money.

I noticed that the teams who followed his advice experienced explosive growth. In fact, the simpler the message, the faster the team would grow. So I took this concept into my next business. Using a three-step plan, we built one of the fastest growing teams in the history of network marketing. Now each time I get asked questions with complicated answers, I go back to our simple message. I usually say, "I'm not sure about that, but I do know that if you will sign up a few distributors, sign up a few customers, and help them do exactly the same thing, you will start making some money with us!"

If you have a tough time explaining it, it will slow down your growth. If others have a tough time understanding it, it will slow down your growth. My rule of thumb is, if an 8-year-old can't do it, then consider not doing it. And if an 8-year-old can't explain it to someone else so that they can understand it, then you probably shouldn't do it either. It's really that simple.

CHAPTER 24

Freedom

On your quest for Beach Money, you will experience the roller-coaster ups and the downs that come with being an entrepreneur. You will grow as you overcome seemingly insurmountable obstacles on your climb up the ladder of success. You will get to celebrate the euphoric highs of reaching new levels of achievement in your life.

Beach Money means different things to different people. Beach Money is a metaphor for freedom. You can be free of the financial worries that most people experience. Beach Money also frees up your time so that you can do what you want to do when you want to do it.

You may choose to spend more time with your family or travel the world. You may want to ski the Alps in Europe or stay overnight in the castles of Scotland.

Can you imagine what it would be like to go back to college and get an advanced degree without having to worry about going to a job? Have you thought about writing your first book? Where would you like to go that would completely inspire you? A Beach Money life is anything you choose. Beach Money is real and it's available to you today.

Here are a few Beach Money truths to consider as you begin to build your dream life:

1. **NO EXPERIENCE NECESSARY** – You don't need any special education or experience to have Beach Money.

2. **A PERFECT BUSINESS** – Network marketing provides

a simple, low-cost, turnkey opportunity for creating Beach Money.

3. **LITTLE TO NO RISK** – Network marketing allows you to be in business without the typical risks associated with starting your own company.

4. **ONGOING RESIDUAL INCOME** – By focusing on an opportunity that pays you over and over for work you do just one time, you can grow a substantial Beach Money income in 2 to 5 years.

5. **YOUR GREATEST GIFT** – Typically your greatest fears and your biggest obstacles represent the hidden opportunities that will lead you to your Beach Money life. Embrace them. Sometimes your gifts won't show up for a few years.

6. **TIME OFF** – You can work for a few years, stop working and continue getting paid long after you have stopped working.

As you begin to focus on these Beach Money truths, opportunities will show up for you that were previously unavailable in your life. From your new point of view, you will recognize the difference between dead-end activities and life-altering opportunities. The main difference between you and those that have achieved true financial freedom is those that have a Beach Money life believed it was possible for them and they held onto that belief for an extended period of time.

THERE IS MORE TO THE BEACH MONEY STORY

The primary reason you read this book was because you are interested in having Beach Money. There is a paradox in this. Just because you want it, focus on it, and pursue it does not guarantee you will have it. Your interest and belief in Beach Money is only part of the equation. You must put as much energy into helping others achieve their Beach Money dreams as you put into achieving yours.

As you train others to believe in themselves, pursue their dreams and take action, you will be planting seeds of hope in them. As they succeed, so will you. In fact the more people that you can help achieve their Beach Money dreams, the closer you will get to yours.

Congratulations on moving one step closer to your Beach Money life.

BONUS CHAPTER

Ask Jordan

Q: Is a six-figure network marketing income really possible?

A: It's just numbers. If the business volume in your organization is consistent with a six-figure income, then you will be making a six-figure income. Our income tends to be a reflection of what we believe we are worth. I have over 100 close friends that make six-figure residual incomes. About 30 make six figures monthly. Up until my early 20s, I had never met anyone that had earned more than $35,000 a year. My highest paying job paid me $28,000 a year. In 1995 I sat at a table with a group of high-paid network marketers and I began to believe it was possible for me. That's when everything changed.

In a world where manned flight was considered impossible, Orville and Wilbur Wright risked their lives and worldwide ridicule to prove what they already knew in their hearts. They wouldn't have done it unless they believed.

Network marketing represents one of the biggest economies in the world doing almost $200 billion per year in revenue. Just like the business of entertainment and professional athletics, the big names make millions. Network Marketing is no different. And each big earner started as a new distributor at some point.

My combined total network marketing income in my first 10 years was $0. Between my 11th year through present, I have earned almost $20 million. And there are many others that have accomplished much more. Yes, big money is possible with belief, vision, focus and hard work.

Q: Why do you love network marketing as a business model?

A: Network marketing offers a business that is open to anyone with no products to purchase, unlimited income potential, no inventory, no deliveries, true residual income, and a business that can be worked from anywhere. I haven't seen anything else that has this much upside for so little downside. Your company does all the heavy lifting and carries most of all the overhead. It's a dream business.

Q: It's clear that I still don't know what I'm doing. Any suggestions for finally mastering network marketing?

A: As I learned the language, distinctions, rules, and skills to master the game of flying helicopters, a whole new world opened up to me. I began to see things for the first time that were once invisible to me. And I now get to experience life from a whole new point of view. The same holds true for you and your network marketing business. If you have never before done network marketing successfully, its because you have not mastered the language, distinction, rules, and skills to the game. It can be exciting and confronting at the same time. It's easy to question and doubt whether it will really work for you. I've had that experience many times on my journey to learning to fly helicopters. I've had to relearn the meaning of digging deep. But on the journey, I get to experience what most people never do. And I get to see things that most people never get to see! Small setbacks and breakthroughs experienced over time lead you down the path of personal growth. As you grow personally, you gain power. That power carries with it the potential to add immense value to the lives of others. And when you do this, your income rises.

Q: What do I say to someone when I first meet them?

A: Focus not on what you will say to them but what you want to learn from them. What to say is about you. What to learn is about them. I recently walked into a Starbucks and I asked the spikey haired dude behind the counter how long he had worked there. He told me he was just doing it for fun and he owned two small "Vape" shops that he hired some other guys to run for him. He then told me his family owns one of the largest nail salon syndicates in the world with over 280 stores. I learned a lot about him in a short conversation. And then I simply said, "We need to get together sometime to kick around some ideas! When you meet someone new, take your time and really get to know THEM first. Keep your business in your bag as something really special to offer only when the time is right.

Q: I have shown the business seven times recently, and have had no sign ups. What could be going on?

A: When this happens to you, you may start to question whether you have lost your touch, whether the marketplace has changed, or whether you just don't have it in you. That's a normal reaction. I have been through dry spells like this more times than I can count. It's frustrating I know, but I also know that if you stay in touch with those people some of them will sign up within a few weeks or months. The key is to not let your dry spells lead you to ruin. Most people get discouraged and stop working. You can't let that happen to you if you want to have a successful business. Keep moving! One time I showed the business to 28 people before getting a sign up. Over time almost 1/2 of the 28 signed up because I didn't quit and I stayed in contact with all of them!

Q: How do I show the business to people if I'm afraid?

A:. Most things that are worthwhile are things that will take you out of your comfort zone. When I was working on getting my helicopter license, most skills I had to learn were way out of my comfort zone and I was afraid to continue at times. But I learned to trust the process. Today the things I was once afraid of are routine. Focus on the end result and the dream you desire and not on what you are afraid of. And you will probably still be afraid. That's normal until you get comfortable. It's the price you pay for achieving your dream.

It's okay. Everyone is afraid when getting started. And sometimes that fear will come and go and even linger for awhile. When you experience fear, attempt to reframe it. See if you can generate some excitement out of your fear or let go of your attachment to the outcome.

When Larry King, the famous talk show host, would interview famous dignitaries, he was blinded by his fear. He would say to himself, "No matter what, I'm not going to die and it will be over in an hour." That would get him through it and in 100% of the cases he would end the interview feeling great about how it went.

These mental strategies can help you get through what may be a terrifying situation. You are not going to die. You get to show something really amazing to people that can change their lives for the better. Lose yourself in the experience and try and have fun. Be bold and breathe confidence into your presentations.

It will get easier over time and you'll look back a year from now and laugh at the absurdity that you were once afraid.

Q: How do I get my unmotivated reps to go to work?

A: Haha. Wish I had an answer for that one! If you want to make real money in your program, let go of the need to pump your people up. Go find people better than you. One third will do nothing. One third will do very little. One third will do a little more than a little and 1 in 30 will typically lead you to an organization of thousands. Don't fight this. Work with it! Go sponsor 1-4 people per month for 2 to 3 years. Give everyone a chance. Train them and give them all the tools. You take two steps for every one they take. But if they are not calling you back or doing anything, go sponsor another one! There are thousands of Michael Jordan's out there that have never picked up a basketball.

Q: I am uncomfortable asking my family and friends about the business because I have tried so many other companies. I'm sure they are thinking, "Oh, here she goes again . . . another scheme!" How do I deal with this? How did you deal with it after you joined your 11th or 12th company?

A: In situations like this I think its best to acknowledge their concerns head on. And then take it away and wait.

"Listen, I know you know me and you know I have been in everything under the sun. And here I go again. You'll expect me to approach you and this time I won't. In fact, I won't say a word unless you ask me. So I think this one is totally different and it's going to be really big . . . but if you want more info, YOU'LL HAVE TO COME TO ME."

Then leave them alone until they can't stand it any more and then they have to ask. You'll want to bring it up but don't. Remain completely silent about your business no matter how bad you want to tell them. And when they ask, don't unload on them. Give them a little. If they start to resist or give you a hard time then take it away again. Get their 100% permission to share before you do. The more you hold back the more they will want to know. Prove to them that this time is different by creating some results worth talking about!

Q: How do you handle when someone said they are interested and then they don't call you back?

A: Most people have full and busy lives filled with distractions. We really rarely know what is going on in someone's life. There are 100 possible reasons why they may not be calling you back. Most importantly don't make it mean anything other than the timing is off. They may have been talked out of it by a friend or relative. They may have recently received some tragic news. They may be on a family trip or feeling excessive financial stress. My advice is to keep them on your list and continue to stay in touch. Don't badger them. Send a card or little gift, place a periodic call, e-mail, etc just to check in. If there is some special update or news from your company, keep them in the loop. At one point they may re-engage but for now chalk it up to "not now, maybe later." For you to have a large and growing networking marketing business, you will have to let go of the attachment to the outcome. It can be frustrating and it takes lots of patience. I have had people vaporize for months at a time and then come back with a vengeance!

Q: I have a little dilemma. After a meeting I did the other night, I had a guy come over to me and say that he was invited by someone in another state that he doesn't know well. He said he is looking for a local sponsor and would like me to sponsor him. I'm a little uncomfortable with doing that but shouldn't he be allowed to choose his own sponsor?

A: As you grow and become more successful in your business, this scenario will become more and more common to you. If you are feeling uncomfortable there is a reason. I have a saying that I adopted from the Founder and President of a major airline. "When in doubt, always do the right thing." What would happen if you sent one of your contacts to a meeting in another state and the presenter sponsored your guest? You would never trust that person ever again! The entire system breaks down when we can't trust each other without the fear of our cross line team mates taking our referred guests. So always do the right thing! Say to that guest, "I can't sponsor you! I can assist you in getting your business going but you were referred by someone else and that person deserves to have you as part of their organization" (personally, I will NEVER sponsor them even if they insist. Once trust is broken it is nearly impossible to rebuild. It's not worth it!) Imagine a large organization where everyone works together. By doing the right thing, you will have hundreds or even thousands of allies working on your behalf. Let's all work for each other and not against each other!

Q: If I want to sign up 3-5 distributors per month for the next 24 months, what would be a good strategy?

A: Well, if your company offers a way that people can try or "sample" the product, I would consider having a month-to-month strategy introducing it to 5 people per week (approximately one per day) It's a three-step system.

1) Ask someone from your list to try the product. 2) Tell them that you will give the sample to them if they agree to watch the video(s) with you present. 3) Ask them to introduce you to one person that would also allow you to give them product to try and watch the video(s). Do this as many times as possible going as deep as possible through referrals until someone says they want to be a distributor (eventually someone says they are interested from watching the videos). You'll get some product users along the way as well. When someone says they are interested in a distributorship, go back up the line and ask each person above that watched the videos and tried the product if they want to be the sponsor of the person saying "yes." And then keep going up. I have put as many as 7 people in a weekend doing this. So over the course of a month you might introduce your business to 20 people doing this. When one says yes, go back up the line and put in everyone who wants to have an instant organization! Do this and teach this every month and watch your business go BOOM!

Q: My Upline isn't working the business anymore. What should I do?

A: Well I would recommend doing the exact same thing you would do if your Upline were working the business. You don't get paid off what your Upline does. You get paid as a result of the customer volume you create in your Downline! Most likely if your Upline quit, they wouldn't have been much use to you anyway! Either way, you're in good company because most successful people in Network Marketing don't have active Uplines. It's YOUR business so I recommend you take FULL responsibility and not use your Upline as your reason to be idle. YOU be the leader. It always starts with you. Time to get to work, fill your calendar and stop using your Upline as a reason to fail. Ouch! You can take it.

Q: I'm not a big dreamer. In all of these network marketing workshops and books they talk about finding the "why that makes you cry." I haven't been able to do this. I want to build a business that will pay me a residual income but I don't have that driving ambition that everyone talks about.

A: This is a "what's wrong with me?" question. Each of us are different. We all have different interests, beliefs, ambitions, and dreams. In fact even the top network marketers in the world aren't driven all the time. So stop beating yourself up and just have fun building your business. No need to make it such a serious thing! Who cares if you cry over your why? It doesn't even matter if you have identified a why or not! You wouldn't be doing it if you didn't have one. My friend Mark Herdering (author of "Hanging Out for a Living" www.hangingoutforaliving.com) wanted to replace his cell phone bill first . . . then his car payment then his rent payment, etc. Today he pays all his bills through his network marketing residual check. I highly doubt if he got teary eyed when he was fantasizing about his Verizon bill being paid for by his residual check. So maybe it's time to lighten up and just have fun doing your business!

Q: I have been with my company for about 6 months and I've only signed up 4 people and nobody is doing anything. I'm not sure I really have what it takes to motivate people. Suggestions?

A: First of all, you are in the same boat as every other network marketer that has ever made money on the planet. All of them at one point had sponsored 4 that did nothing. In fact, statistically, most people find that their magic number seems to happen between 20 and 30 personally sponsored distributors. You may get lucky and sign up a mover and a shaker early on, but most people don't. You have to pay your dues. Everyone has the same opportunity to win but few will play the game long enough. Actually, in most cases, your runners won't be brought in by you. They'll come in on your 3rd, 4th, or 5th level. Don't get discouraged. In my previous company I didn't find anyone that wanted to go to work until my 16th distributor on my 20th month. So the plan becomes figuring out how many people you'll need to show it to to sponsor enough people that will go out and do it. I have found that on average, for every 20-30 people you sponsor into your business, you'll find ONE that is really serious and will go to town with it. So how fast do you want to get there?

Sponsor 4 per month and you'll find one in 4 to 6 months. Sponsor 1 per month and it may take you 2 years. You decide. Now you'll make good part-time money along the way but the big bucks are reserved for those that can run the course and see the job through. If it were that easy, they wouldn't pay us the big money when we get there! Oh did you notice that I said nothing about "motivating" your people? That's because it's not really a variable of your success. Stick with finding the right people at the right time.

Q: How can I get it to grow faster?

A: First understand "it" doesn't grow. People do! Your group consists of people working because they want to better their lives and customers using your product or service! So when people are inspired to action you'll experience growth!

Let's say you have this beautiful tree that is growing a little each week. You want it to grow faster so you try a new type of plant food. That doesn't make it grow faster so you try digging it up and replanting it in another pot. That flops so you experiment by putting the pot in a new location. The plant loses half it's leaves. You try extra water and a little more plant food. Then you replant it again. It loses the rest of its leaves and you begin to wonder why. Were you doing the wrong thing by giving it extra water and plant food? Did you mess up by replanting it twice? The experts told you that you needed it to grow faster! Did they lie to you? No!! Under certain circumstances you did the right thing. However, your results would have been much better if you had been patient and stuck to the plan of the fundamentals of plant care.

Q: How do I get my family to see this?

A: Most importantly, don't try and get your family to "see it" if they're not ready. If you force it on them you'll drive them further away. Don't push them or argue with them. That will make things much worse. Give them space. It may take time. Have patience.

If your spouse is resistant, then let him/her open and cash your checks for awhile even if they are small. It can be a challenge if your family is not supportive. But it's not the end of the road. Ask for what you want but try and be understanding if they are not supportive. Let them know that your intention is to earn their support and that your intention is to provide a better life for the family.

Q: Who should I target in my recruiting efforts?

A: "Targeting" is a term that comes from the traditional business world. There are two problems with targeting a certain type of person in network marketing. The first problem is, the people you think will do it won't and the people you don't think will do it will. The second problem is, you never know who someone will lead you to. Targeting people in network marketing is generally a bad idea. You'll discover that people you were pretty sure would do nothing go on to build substantial organizations. And I've had some really awful business builders lead me to some incredible leaders. Don't pre-judge. Even people that don't like people know other people that don't like people and many of them will love your product! The only thing I look for is someone who is open and a little hungry. But if given a choice, I'd prefer to speak with connected, positive, and entrepreneurial-minded people. Hmmmm. Maybe that's who you should "target."

Q: People seem to resist me when I try and set up an appointment. Any suggestions?

A: Have you ever walked into a glass door that wasn't open?

Ouch! That's kind of what happens when we try and present our opportunity to someone who is not OPEN to take a look. If the door is open, then we can simply step in. If it's closed but we see someone behind the glass we can ask, "Are you open?" If they say, "yes," we can step right in. Glass is invisible and its easy to walk into so it helps to ask whether the door is open or closed. If the door is closed, then be prepared to walk into the glass if you try and present without permission to enter! So just ask the question, "Are you open?"

Q: I brought in my first 3 distributors and I'm trying to get them motivated. It's been 2 months and they haven't done anything. What can I do to motivate them?"

A: Trying to motivate your distributors is a formula for burnout. Everyone will do the business or not based on where they are in their lives at any given time. Just encourage and inform them. Make them aware of upcoming events and conferences and invite them to call in to weekly conference calls. And then you keep sponsoring until you find some that don't need any motivation.

Do what you want your distributors to do. Keep sponsoring new people and encourage others to participate. That's all you need to do. Stop trying to motivate people. Even if you are superman or woman, you will most likely fail at getting your people to go to work. Our job is not to turn our people into us. Our job is to find people better than us.

Building the business means working to get the opportunity in front of NEW PEOPLE. If someone is ready, they will step into it. If they are not ready, no amount of convincing or coercing will get them to go to work. If your team members are not responding, then sponsor five to ten more over the next few months.

Q: What does success look like for a new distributor?

A: Success is different for each distributor. I think true success is felt when challenges are overcome and progress is made. When someone experiences a breakthrough and then experiences growth, they feel successful. For example, when a new distributor sponsors a new distributor or signs up a new customer, they feel success. When someone reaches a new lifestyle goal or achieves their next promotion, they feel success. So reaching a new milestone is always a representation of growth which translates into success. This year I had four helicopter goals and each time I accomplish one I feel success. For example one goal was to take friends in the helicopter on my own over the mountains to death valley for lunch. I have taken a few trips so far with friends and that feels like success because I achieved the goal. I also had a goal to fly a turbine helicopter. I planned it, scheduled it, paid for it, and then a few weeks ago did it! That created the feeling of success.

Q: In this business, what do you see are the biggest challenges for any distributor?

A: The biggest challenge is mindset first and then skills. The skills are relatively easy to learn fairly quickly. The shifting of disempowering values, beliefs, and philosophies are the toughest challenge. Usually a shift in focus can open up the floodgates to success. My objective is usually to get a distributor to see something they could not see before. Challenges are rarely an issue of skill.

Most challenges are overcome by releasing past disempowering beliefs.

Q: If my company lowered the price to get in I could build much faster! Why do network marketing companies charge so much to sign up?

A: Think about what someone gets when they buy your business. Make a list. Present each benefit slowly so your potential distributor really understands what they are getting. $500-$5000 is a small start-up fee for a business that can produce a significant passive residual income. The potential is greater than most traditional businesses that cost $100,000 to over $1 million to start. Plus it can be started part-time without having to hire employees with no limit to growth. A $500 a month income ($6000 per year) is a 600% return on a $1000 start up. Most businesses take years to break even! In Network Marketing you risk little and can potentially be profitable your first month, not to mention the business education one receives from leaders that have actually built something significant. True, there are no guarantees but compared to other options the start-up costs weighted against the income potential and possible lifestyle is off the charts. I would challenge you to find any traditional business costing $1,000,000 or more to start that has the potential to throw off a $100,000 per month in residual walk away, Beach Money income! $500 to $5000 is a small price to pay

Q: When is it time to throw in the towel?

A:"The essence of bravery is the unwillingness to give up on something or someone" - UNKNOWN AUTHOR

I don't know if I'm brave or not, but I can name the names of 1000 people that gave up on themselves before I gave up on them. And I'm still here 10 years later standing for them when they are ready to start believing in themselves again.

After "trying" and failing at 11 companies in 10 years, I finally figured out that I was the reason for the failure. It wasn't the product. All the companies had great products. It wasn't the compensation plan. There were people making money in all the companies. It wasn't the leadership. Each company had great leaders. I had lessons to learn before I deserved success. Until I redefined my focus, and buried my past "stories" that were holding me back, history kept repeating itself! I was tired of bouncing around from company to company. Read five biographies written by successful entrepreneurs and you'll find that they all re-invented themselves and their companies repeatedly until they got it right. If you are looking for a lottery ticket, then go buy a lottery ticket! This is business and successful business means persisting through the ups and the downs until you get it right. For example, let's say you want to get in physical shape but you have a problem with quitting and persisting. So you join a gym and rarely go. Then you get frustrated because you are not getting physically fit. So you quit and join another gym. After 6 years you have joined 3 gyms and you are still weak and flabby. Changing gyms is not the solution. Developing a fresh focus and new habits would be a good start! Trying different companies until you make money is not the answer. Seldom is switching companies the best solution. There are some rare instances that switching to a new company is the right choice but there are many things to consider. If you have an active team, there is no easy way to exit without causing a lot of trouble for others. You will lose face and you will compromise your integrity in the process. And I have found that there is no way around this. There is a price to pay. I have personally found that choosing to become a partner committed to growing the company or going down with the ship is the best overall strategy for LONG-TERM success. You can not succeed with one foot in and one foot out. A leader is one who holds the vision for the team through the calm seas and the rough storms. Are you up for being a leader?

Q: Tell the truth. What does it really take to build a $100,000 a month income.

A: Four things ... 1) Belief. 2) Connections. 3) Massive Action. 4) Timing.

It will be the hardest and most rewarding thing you have ever done in your life. It happens at the moment you take the gloves off and go "all in." It's when you shed your concerns about what other people think. It's when you realize that YOU are the cause of the success of your company and that it's not a lottery. It's when you realize that it's a simple equation that just requires a will to win backed by massive action. A $100,000+ a month income is reserved for those that can reframe the toughest challenges and find the opportunities in them. If you don't have connections, realize that neither did anyone else when they started. There is no room for doubt. Doubt kills dreams.

Massive action means 3-5 presentations a day for awhile ... not forever, just for awhile.

If that seems like a lot, then $100K per month is not for you right now. That's just what it takes. Timing is important but it's not what you think. Timing is created by your vision, your faith, and an idea whose time has come. I have over 100 personal friends that have done it and therefore I know you can to. Whether you will do it is up to you. Oh . . . one more thing. Those that get the big prize are those that would let NOTHING stop them. Quitting is not part of the equation. In other words, there is no stop until the job is done. In the words of billionaire, Kenny Troutt, "See the job through."

Q: As a leader, I make a much smaller amount when someone in my group promotes. Seems counterproductive. Why should I help people promote when I'll ultimately make LESS money??

A: I was told early on that I should work to push the big money into the hands of the newer people. In other words, give the newer people a reason to keep working. In real terms, this means working within the groups of the healthy organizations assisting them with their promotions. I was told I would get wealthy off the leftovers (which is the small difference between the total leadership commission and what they receive). And then teach the team to do the exact same thing! Most people spend so much time chasing the big money that they forget that the big money is in the small money. So they jump around chasing the dollars hoping that someday they'll get rich not realizing that the big money is really in the dimes!

Going after the dollars is the strategy of a linear thinker. It's trading time for money. Not bad if you want to continue to have to work hard all your life. The wealthiest people almost always make the smallest percentage of the total revenue collected. Ray Kroc's family only gets paid a few pennies on each burger sold. But they got wealthy making sure that the franchisees got the bulk of it!

Remember what J. Paul Getty said,

"I would rather have 1% of 100 people's efforts than 100% of my own!"

Q: I am growing as a person each week by listening to material and advice that my amazing mentors have given me. They have been my biggest support. My biggest problem is that I am only 20 years old and I feel like I don't have enough credibility when talking with potential prospects. As a young lady, I often feel like I won't be taken seriously and feel like people will only see me as a girl suckered into a "pyramid scheme." Any advice on how I can improve my credibility and posture?

A: Everyone has their story . . . and the story empowers them, keeps them right where they are, or cripples them completely. Your story is true! And as long as you continue to own it, you'll continue to struggle. The fact is there are many young entrepreneurs in their twenties that have built very large and successful businesses. They each had a different story than yours! The internet revolution was created by kids in their twenties! Some became billionaires. Use that to your advantage! Most kids don't want to be like their parents. For the first time in history, adults are going to the kids for advice on business. So how can you position yourself as a brilliant young entrepreneur with vision for your generation to not be like their parents and work for 40 years to end up broke?

Q: Do you believe in multiple streams of income?

A: I make my money through network marketing. It offers the ultimate in time leverage which is the key to financial freedom. Instead of putting the money I make into a bank account or CD paying 1-2% interest, I buy bank-owned Real Estate and get renters. I use property managers. I'll buy a bank-owned home in the city for $5000 and then renovate it for $20,000. It will appraise for $50,000 to $110,000. I can then rent it for $1000/mo with a 50% cash-on-cash return plus $25,000-$85,000 instant equity. Network Marketing gives me a the cash to do deals like this.

I don't think working multiple network marketing opportunities works well because your time is too divided and you'll have a tough time succeeding at anything. But you will need a place to put your network marketing income as you make it so educate yourself on investment opportunities that will help you keep and grow your net worth.

Recommended Reading

How to Get Absolutely Anything You Want: In Six Practical Doable, Time Tested Steps by Margie Aliprandi

MLM Blueprint™:Your Subconscious Journey to Network Marketing Success by Kody Bateman

Promptings by Kody Bateman

The Four Year Career for Women by Kimmy Brooke

Mach II With Your Hair on Fire and *The Four Year Career* by Richard Bliss Brooke

The Four Year Career by Richard Bliss Brooke

How to Win Friends & Influence People by Dale Carnegie

Fearless Networking by Todd Falcone

The 45 Second Presentation That Will Change Your Life by Don Failla

The Greatest Networker in the World by John Milton Fogg

Making the First Circle Work by Randy Gage

25 to Life by Adam Green

Right or Almost Right by John Haremza

The Magic of Compound Recruiting by Hubert H. Humphrey

Rich Dad, Poor Dad by Robert T. Kiyosaki

The Millionaire Maker's Guide for Creating a Cash Machine for Life by Loral Langemeier

Swim with the Sharks Without Being Eaten Alive by Harvey B. Mackay

The Harvey Mackay Rolodex Network Builder by Harvey B. Mackay

The Choice by Og Mandino

Truth or Delusion by Ivan R. Misner

The Slight Edge by Jeff Olson

Brains on Fire by Robbin Phillips, Greg Cordell, Geno Church, Spike Jones

The Next Millionaires by Paul Zane Pilzer

Rock your Network Marketing Business by Sarah Robbins

Mindset Before Matter for your Network Marketing Journey by David Ross

Start with Why by Simon Sinek

Big Al Tells All by Tom "Big Al" Schreiter

Yes, Sometimes It Is About the Money by Steve Schulz

The Magic of Thinking Big by David J. Schwartz

The Game of Networking by Rob Sperry

Be, Do and Have More by Presley Swagerty

The Referral of a Lifetime by Tim Templeton, Ken Blanchard, and Lynda Stephenson

GoPro by Eric Worre

Quotes and Confirmations by Beyond Wynn

Your First Year in Network Marketing by Mark Yarnell and Rene Reid Yarnell

Beach Money: Creating Your Dream Life Through Network Marketing,

is also available as an eBook, as a CD set, or audio download.

CPSIA information can be obtained
at www.ICGtesting.com
Printed in the USA
BVHW041629020820
585229BV00010B/28

9 781628 654493